DAVID WILLIAMSON's first full-length play, *The Coming of Stork*, premiered at the La Mama Theatre, Carlton, in 1970 and later became the film *Stork*, directed by Tim Burstall.

The Removalists and *Don's Party* followed in 1971, then *Jugglers Three* (1972), *What If You Died Tomorrow?* (1973), *The Department* (1975), *A Handful of Friends* (1976), *The Club* (1977) and *Travelling North* (1979). In 1972 *The Removalists* won the Australian Writers' Guild AWGIE Award for best stage play and the best script in any medium and the British production saw Williamson nominated most promising playwright by the London *Evening Standard*.

The 1980s saw his success continue with *Celluloid Heroes* (1980), *The Perfectionist* (1982), *Sons of Cain* (1985), *Emerald City* (1987) and *Top Silk* (1989); whilst the 1990s produced *Siren* (1990), *Money and Friends* (1991), *Brilliant Lies* (1993), *Sanctuary* (1994), *Dead White Males* (1995), *Heretic* (1996), *Third World Blues* (an adaptation of *Jugglers Three*) and *After the Ball* (both in 1997), and *Corporate Vibes* and *Face to Face* (both in 1999). *The Great Man* (2000), *Up for Grabs*, *A Conversation*, *Charitable Intent* (all in 2001), *Soulmates* (2002) and *Birthrights* (2003) have since followed.

Williamson is widely recognised as Australia's most successful playwright and over the last thirty years his plays have been performed throughout Australia and produced in Britain, United States, Canada and many European countries. A number of his stage works have been adapted for the screen, including *The Removalists, Don's Party, The Club, Travelling North, Emerald City, Sanctuary* and *Brilliant Lies*.

David Williamson has won the Australian Film Institute film script award for *Petersen* (1974), *Don's Party* (1976), *Gallipoli* (1981) and *Travelling North* (1987) and has won eleven Australian Writers' Guild AWGIE Awards. He lives on Queensland's Sunshine Coast with his writer wife, Kristin Williamson.

DAVID WILLIAMSON

BIRTHRIGHTS
SOULMATES

TWO PLAYS

CURRENCY PRESS, SYDNEY

CURRENCY PLAYS

Birthrights and *Soulmates* first published in 2003
by Currency Press Pty Ltd,
PO Box 2287, Strawberry Hills, NSW, 2012, Australia
enquiries@currency.com.au
www.currency.com.au

Copyright © David Williamson, 2003

COPYING FOR EDUCATIONAL PURPOSES
The Australian *Copyright Act 1968* (Act) allows a maximum of one chapter or 10% of this book, whichever is the greater, to be copied by any educational institution for its educational purposes provided that that educational institution (or the body that administers it) has given a remuneration notice to Copyright Agency Limited (CAL) under the Act.

For details of the CAL licence for educational institutions contact CAL, 19/157 Liverpool Street, Sydney, NSW, 2000. Tel: (02) 9394 7600; Fax: (02) 9394 7601; E-mail: info@copyright.com.au

COPYING FOR OTHER PURPOSES
Except as permitted under the Act, for example a fair dealing for the purposes of study, research, criticism or review, no part of this book may be reproduced, stored in a retrieval system, or transmitted in any form or by any means without prior written permission. All inquiries should be made to the publisher at the address above.

Any performance or public reading of *Birthrights* or *Soulmates* is forbidden unless a licence has been received from the author or the author's agent. The purchase of this book in no way gives the purchaser the right to perform the play in public, whether by means of a staged production or a reading. All applications for public performance should be addressed to the playwright c/- Cameron Creswell Management, Suite 5, Edgecliff Court, 2 New McLean Street, Edgecliff NSW, 2027, Australia.

In accordance with the requirement of the Australian Media, Entertainment & Arts Alliance, Currency Press has made every effort to identify, and gain permission of, the artists who appear in the photographs which illustrate these plays.

NATIONAL LIBRARY OF AUSTRALIA CIP DATA

    Williamson, David, 1942–.
        Birthrights; Soulmates: two plays.
        ISBN 0 86819 698 3.
        I. Williamson, David, 1942– Soulmates. II. Title. III. Title: Soulmates.
    A822.3

Set by Dean Nottle
Cover design by Kate Florance
Front cover shows William Zappa as Danny and Jacki Weaver as Heather in the 2002 Sydney Theatre Company production. Photo: Tracey Schramm.
Back cover shows Kate Raison as Helen and Michelle Doake as Claudia in the 2003 Ensemble Theatre production. Photo: Melinda Koutchavlis.

Contents

BIRTHRIGHTS	1
Introduction	
David Williamson	*3*
Act One	9
Act Two	43
SOULMATES	79
Introduction	
Kathy Lette	*81*
Act One	85
Act Two	119

Currency Press acknowledges the Traditional Owners of the Country on which we live and work. We pay our respects to all Aboriginal and Torres Strait Islander Elders, past and present.

BIRTHRIGHTS

Asher Keddie (left) as Kelly and Maria Theodorakis as Claudia in the 2003 Melbourne Theatre Company production. (Photo: Jeff Busby)

Introduction

David Williamson

Some years ago a good friend in her late 30s, with a successful career in mid flight, suddenly felt a strong urge to have a child. She and her partner were unable to conceive and IVF became her only option. Desperate to have a child, she went through what she now refers to as IVF hell. And it can be a hell on many levels. It offers a promise of parenthood which all too often it doesn't deliver. It pumps a woman so full of fertility hormones that her body tells her she must be pregnant when in fact she's not, which creates deep moods of depression and a sense of failure. Our friend became increasingly obsessed and determined to have a child. When cycle after cycle of IVF failed she often found herself experiencing unexplained rage.

In an email she sent when I was researching my play *Birthrights* she said, 'I suddenly realised all my friends who had protested so fiercely against the constraints of childrearing had somehow managed to slip one in. I felt terribly betrayed. Then I realised that everyone had children and in fact I remember the day it dawned on me. That is what human beings do. They have children.'

She has now come to terms, more or less, with the fact that she will never have a child, and her life is once again full and productive, but it took many years for her to begin to recover.

But I didn't start *Birthrights* because of what this friend had been through. Stories often stare me in the face for ages before I realise they are there. I'd been reading headlines about clashes between football coaches and administrations for years in the 1970s before it dawned on me that here the seeds of drama were screaming to be noticed. That play became *The Club*.

To find what started *Birthrights* I looked back at the notes which I typically make before I start writing. One of the very first jottings was, 'Show how men's status, striving and competitiveness cut them off from full humanity'.

I'm sure that's still in the play somewhere, but I'm not quite sure how I got from a theme of quintessential male angst to the problems of two sisters whose lives are altered forever when one, in a burst of generosity and compassion, agrees to become artificially inseminated and have a child for her older, infertile sister.

I suspect I drifted from a play about male problems to one about female dilemmas because I started to realise that in an era in which traditional sex roles are dissolving, the problems and life choices of females are often more acute, complex and dramatically interesting than those of males.

In a society in which the great majority of women work either full-time or part-time, there is nothing more troubling and perplexing for many women than the decision about whether and when to have children.

Yet despite the difficulties, many women like my friend still want to have babies and some want them very badly indeed. And it's becoming increasingly more difficult for them to achieve this aim. In an ideal world their male partners would do half their share of the children's upbringing and household work, but survey after survey shows that this ideal world has not arrived yet and it may never arrive. Women know that in a certain sense they are the ones who will be left holding the baby.

Add to this the fact that they're going to get little help in the areas of childcare from either government or employer, and the increasing reluctance of males to take on the responsibilities of fatherhood, and the baby question can start to get daunting. Even with caring partners and a flexible workforce, the problems aren't necessarily over. Many couples who turn out to be infertile have to turn to IVF.

This, I suspect, is where my story really began. I started to think of the IVF hell my friend went through and what the complications would be if a female partner of my male character was attempting to have a baby this way.

But I didn't want a play that was solely about IVF and the emotional roller coaster it engenders. As always, I wanted a play about the sometimes delicate and sometimes brutal dance of clashing human egos precariously held in check by the need to be respected and loved, or out of a need to avoid causing others pain.

I started researching the general field of surrogacy and came across cases of sisters donating eggs for IVF to infertile sisters, of women being surrogate mothers for their sister's fertilised eggs, and of women actually conceiving and bearing babies for their sisters through insemination using the sister's husband's sperm. What initially attracted me was the selflessness and generosity often associated with the act, and then I became intrigued by the ethical and emotional complexities that followed from it.

I began to envisage a character who, in her late 30s, had to resort fruitlessly to IVF, but who had many years before got effortlessly pregnant by direct insemination in order to give her infertile older sister the baby she craved. Wouldn't her sadness be even more intense when she realised that she had given away, out of generosity, the only child she was ever going to bear? What if my fictional character Claudia had already become very fond of her biological daughter, Kelly, years before realising she is never going to have a child of her own? Would she want Kelly to know the truth? Would it be a good thing for Kelly to know the truth? Would her sister Helen feel threatened by the possibility?

Then there was the question of how relevant the actual biological parent was, in any case. If we are all totally products of our environment, as many believe, then genes should count for little. The parents who bring up the child would be the only influence on its development.

But the more I researched, the more it became apparent that knowing the truth about biological parentage is extremely important for many people. Adopted children often go to extraordinary lengths to find their real parents; similarly adults who have adopted their children out often desperately want to locate the children they feel they have lost. The whole tragic saga of the stolen generation shows how potent the question of biological parentage can be.

And it makes sense. Parents have always known that one baby can be cross and irritable, another shy, and another fearless to the point of distraction. Modern research is verifying what parents have always suspected: children inherit more than just physiques and facial features. A complex interaction between our genetic legacy and our environment makes us what we are. Aspects of our very core nature can be sheeted back to our unique DNA code, and the urge to find out the truth about our biological legacy seems to be a result of that intuitively-grasped fact.

Would Claudia become very fond of her biological child Kelly, seeing in her features, gestures and wilful impetuosity the legacy of her own genes? And would she start to compete, despite herself, for her biological daughter's affection? Even if Claudia had no intention of ever displacing her sister Helen, might she still not want to be acknowledged as part author of the DNA blueprint that had, in the miraculous way that genes and environment interact, become Kelly?

In these days when intellectual property has become a huge issue, the densest and most complex piece of information we own is our own DNA code. My research indicated that it's hard to give that away to someone else and not remain interested in what becomes of it.

And therein, I hope, lies drama.

Sunshine Beach
April 2003

Birthrights was first produced by Melbourne Theatre Company at the Playhouse, Victorian Arts Centre, on 16 April 2003, with the following cast:

HELEN DEAKIN	Doris Younane
CLAUDIA McADAM	Maria Theodorakis
MARTIN	Peter Houghton
MARK	Kevin Harrington
MARGARET McADAM	Deidre Rubenstein
KELLY	Asher Keddie

Director, Tom Gutteridge
Designer, Louise McCarthy
Lighting Designer, David Walters
Sound Designer, David Franzke

The play was first produced in Sydney by the Ensemble Theatre at the Playhouse, Sydney Opera House, on 3 June 2003, with the following cast:

HELEN DEAKIN	Kate Raison
CLAUDIA McADAM	Michelle Doake
MARTIN	Glenn Hazeldine
MARK	Andrew Doyle
MARGARET McADAM	Lorraine Bayly
KELLY	Katharine Jones

Director, Sandra Bates
Assistant Director, Andrew Doyle
Designer, Colin Mitchell
Lighting Designer, Shane Stevens
Stage Manager, Kathy Munro

CHARACTERS

HELEN DEAKIN
CLAUDIA McADAM
MARTIN
MARK
MARGARET McADAM
KELLY

ACT ONE

SCENE ONE

Prince of Wales Hospital. Sydney. 1983.

HELEN, *29, lies in a hospital bed. She looks up as her sister,* CLAUDIA, *25, enters the room and moves towards her and smiles.*

CLAUDIA: How are you feeling?
HELEN: Awful.

    CLAUDIA *sits down. There's a silence.*

CLAUDIA: Mark said there may be a problem...
HELEN: *May* be a problem? I'm never going to have a child. Didn't he tell you that?
CLAUDIA: He said he'd let you tell me the details.
HELEN: No eggs. Simple as that. Premature Ovarian Failure.
CLAUDIA: What causes that?
HELEN: They don't know. Thyroid deficiency, childhood mumps, a misspent youth.
CLAUDIA: Misspent youth?
HELEN: Sexually transmitted disease is one possible cause.
CLAUDIA: You didn't have any disease.
HELEN: Actually I did.
CLAUDIA: When.
HELEN: When you were thirteen or fourteen.
CLAUDIA: What kind of disease?

    HELEN *looks at her and claps her hands together.* CLAUDIA *raises her eyebrows.*

HELEN: The karate champion? Turns out he was even more promiscuous than I was.
CLAUDIA: Come on. You weren't exactly a nymphomaniac.
HELEN: No, but I don't think it was just my 'outgoing personality' that kept the phones ringing.

CLAUDIA: How come I didn't know?

HELEN: Mother hustled me off to the clinic to make sure no hint of this reached your virginal ears.

CLAUDIA: Did they really say that was the likely cause?

HELEN: No, they took enormous pains to say it almost certainly wasn't, which means of course it almost certainly was.

CLAUDIA: Helen, it's just the patriarchal medical profession trying to load you up with guilt because you had a perfectly normal interest in sex.

HELEN: Whatever. The fact is I'm barren. Sterile.

CLAUDIA: You can adopt. Julie Travers says it's just as good as having your own.

HELEN: It took them four years and you can't get kids from Korea anymore.

There's a silence.

CLAUDIA: More and more women are choosing not to have children these days.

HELEN: Well, I'm not one of them. When that bloody maternal thing kicks in, it kicks in. You can't just say: 'Hell, no more of that'. I know *you've* made it perfectly clear you're never having any—

CLAUDIA: I didn't say I wasn't *ever* going to have them.

HELEN: Yes you did.

CLAUDIA: I said I wanted to establish my career first.

HELEN: You said late thirties at the earliest, and probably never. I was so upset I cried half that night.

CLAUDIA: I wasn't attacking you and Mark.

HELEN: Yes you were. You said Mark just wanted a corporate wife stroke incubator.

CLAUDIA: I wouldn't have said that.

HELEN: Yes you did.

CLAUDIA: I must've been drunk.

HELEN: You were. Drunk and arrogant. How you were going to be a senior partner in your law firm before you were thirty-five and what a tragedy it was that I'd wasted my brains and become a doormat. Mark was furious.

CLAUDIA: I felt a lot of that baby obsession was coming from him.

HELEN: No!

ACT ONE

CLAUDIA: Wanted his brilliant genes copied as many times as possible.

HELEN: You're totally wrong. You're just so anti-baby that you don't even want to try and understand.

CLAUDIA: That's not— [true].

HELEN: I know it makes no rational sense whatsoever, but you can't just wish it away! You want to feel its skin, smell its smell, have its little fingers clutching you.

Tears form in HELEN*'s eyes.*

CLAUDIA: I'm sorry. I didn't come here to make you upset.

HELEN *tries to control her tears.*

All I was trying to say is that a life without children can be just as rich and rewarding as—

HELEN: You have *no* idea, do you? No idea. Just like our mother: 'You'll just have to accept it and get on with your life'.

CLAUDIA: She was just trying to be realistic.

HELEN: Realistic? Try totally insensitive. As always.

CLAUDIA: Sorry, I didn't come in here to upset you.

HELEN: You and that new boyfriend of yours are just so smug. Just so smug.

CLAUDIA: Helen—

HELEN: Never hear the end of your 'great plans for the future'. Waterfront apartments. Films, theatre. Never cook, always eat out. Live in Europe. It's just so hollow. So selfish. Can't either of you see that?

CLAUDIA: [*getting irritated*] I just don't see my future as being an incubator for some man's genes.

HELEN: Your own genes too. Does your bloody feminism ever consider that? Your genes too. If we're not here to bring life into the world then what the hell are we here for? Yuppie self indulgence?

CLAUDIA: Don't get upset.

HELEN: How can I *not* get upset?! Wouldn't you be if the one thing you really wanted in life was suddenly snatched away from you? Wouldn't you be?

She breaks down and sobs uncontrollably. CLAUDIA *holds her with genuine concern.*

I'm sorry. I just can't think rationally right now. The whole rest of my life was planned and children were such a big part of it.

CLAUDIA: I know.

HELEN *sobs violently.* CLAUDIA *hugs her. The sobs start to subside.*

I could do it.

HELEN: Do what?

CLAUDIA: Have your child.

HELEN *stares at her.* CLAUDIA *warms to the idea.*

Anonymous sperm donor.

HELEN: Don't be crazy.

CLAUDIA: We share half our genes.

HELEN: Claudie, don't say things like that.

CLAUDIA: I mean it.

HELEN: It'd totally mess up your life.

CLAUDIA: For God's sake. I've just turned twenty-five. It'd be fine.

HELEN: I couldn't *possibly* ask you to do it.

CLAUDIA: You didn't ask. I offered.

HELEN: Claudia, no.

CLAUDIA: It's not *that* big a deal.

HELEN: It's a *huge* deal. It's so wonderful for you to even think of it, but it's not something I could ask of anyone.

CLAUDIA: I'm not anyone.

HELEN: Claudia please. You're only making things worse.

HELEN *sobs again.* CLAUDIA *holds her tighter.*

SCENE TWO

Claudia's apartment. Next day.

It's small, inner-city and grotty. Location Rozelle. A start-of-career-type apartment. CLAUDIA *and her new partner* MARTIN *are painting the walls with rollers.*

ACT ONE

MARTIN: It just seems mad to be paying two lots of rent.

CLAUDIA: Martin, I do love you, but I'm not sure about this. The last time I tried living with someone it ended in disaster.

MARTIN: I do all your renovations and you piss me off. Great.

CLAUDIA: I'm not worried about you. I'm worried about me. I'm not easy to live with.

MARTIN: Volatility is a pre-requisite for great sex.

CLAUDIA: Volatility? When I get home from work, try prickly irritation or dull rage.

MARTIN: [*shrugging*] We could try S and M.

CLAUDIA: Believe me, after work I'm someone you approach at great risk.

MARTIN: That law firm exploits you. You work *crazy* hours.

CLAUDIA: How else would the partners have six-figure incomes and play golf on Wednesday?

MARTIN: Why put yourself through it?

CLAUDIA: Clock up enough billing hours and they finally have to make you a partner. Even if you're a woman.

MARTIN: Look, if you're a total nightmare, I'll be out of here. Don't worry.

CLAUDIA: That's exactly why I *am* worried.

MARTIN: Don't be. You could have the charm level of a constipated tree sloth and still be sexy.

CLAUDIA: You really know how to flatter a girl.

She kisses him then breaks away as she remembers something.

Got to phone Helen.

MARTIN: You phoned her half an hour ago.

CLAUDIA: She's close to suicidal.

MARTIN: I'd be throwing a party.

CLAUDIA: Martin.

MARTIN: You put your life on hold for a bellowing little shitting machine, who turns around at eighteen and tells you you're a stupid old fart. And it's cost you ten trips around the world for the privilege. I'm serious. If I was her I'd be throwing a party.

CLAUDIA: Well, you're not her. Having kids has been her obsession. My first memory is her shoving this vile plastic doll at me that shrieked 'Mama'.

MARTIN: Okay, it's rough for her, but there's nothing you can do.
CLAUDIA: Actually there is.
MARTIN: What?
CLAUDIA: I could have one for her.

    MARTIN *stares at her.*

MARTIN: Of all the stupid ideas I've ever heard, that probably wins.
CLAUDIA: We're very close, Martin. When I was a kid I'd take all my problems to her, not Mum.
MARTIN: That doesn't mean you have to have a kid for her.
CLAUDIA: There are some things you feel you've got to do that don't make any rational sense, and this is one of them.
MARTIN: You keep saying you can't *stand* your sister these days.
CLAUDIA: I can't stand what Mark is turning her into.
MARTIN: Helen's *asked* you to do this?
CLAUDIA: No. She says she won't let me do it.

Maria Theodorakis as Claudia and Peter Houghton as Martin in the 2003 Melbourne Theatre Company production. (Photo: Jeff Busby)

MARTIN: Thank God for that.

CLAUDIA: But I know she really wants me to. I've got to call her.

    CLAUDIA *hurries offstage.* MARTIN *watches her go.*

SCENE THREE

Mark's office. City. Two weeks later.

MARK, *35, Helen's husband, is on two phones.*

MARK: [*into the phone*] Hang on, Joyce. [*Into the mobile*] Listen, mate, I'll call you back... when I can! [*He hangs up the mobile. Into the phone*] Joyce, I'm in a meeting, but if Tony rings...

    He looks up as CLAUDIA *enters his office and hangs up the phone. He gets up smiling and motions her to a seat.*

Thanks for coming.

CLAUDIA: How's Helen today?

MARK: A total mess. I know your mother told her to pull herself together and get on with life, but it ain't that easy.

CLAUDIA: She's still really bad?

MARK: Shocking. Never seen her worse. I know children aren't your thing—

CLAUDIA: [*overlapping*] Well, one day / perhaps.

MARK: [*overlapping*] — / but your sister is totally wrecked. And to be truthful, I'm wrecked too. I sit here and wonder what I'm doing spending fourteen hours a day battling my guts out to build up this business. The end point of the exercise was security for my family.

    The phone rings. MARK *picks it up, irritated.*

Joyce, I thought I told you to hold all calls? [*Pause.*] Oh. Right. Put him on. [*Bellowing*] Tony, what the fuck is going on? Our lawyers have been negotiating for three fucking weeks at a billion dollars an hour. You want this deal to happen or not? [*Pause.*] Okay. Deadline twelve o'clock tomorrow and Tony— I mean it. [*He slams down the phone. To* CLAUDIA] Sorry.

CLAUDIA: I'm sorry. About Helen. And for you.

MARK: It's bloody awful.

CLAUDIA: I read about a couple like you and they got a lot of satisfaction by funding an orphanage in India.

MARK: Yeah. Look, straight to the point.

The phone rings. He picks it up angrily.

Joyce! No calls! Oh, right. [*Pause.*] Tony?! [*He listens.*] No! Twelve noon. That's it. [*He slams the phone down. To* CLAUDIA] There's no decency left in the world, Claudia. At every turn they try and screw you. [*Pause.*] You mentioned a possibility to Helen.

CLAUDIA: She said no.

MARK: It was a very, very generous offer, and we were both very moved. But Helen's right. It's far too bloody generous.

CLAUDIA: She can't have a child. I can.

MARK: [*shaking his head*] It's not that simple.

CLAUDIA *looks at him puzzled.*

SCENE FOUR

Martin and Claudia's place. Later.

MARTIN: He wasn't serious?

CLAUDIA: He was.

MARTIN: That's outrageous. What does he think? Money can buy him anything.

CLAUDIA: I'd already offered to do it for free. It's just that for someone with his mindset generosity doesn't compute.

MARTIN: Your sister *does* want to do this now?

CLAUDIA: Yes. If I get paid.

MARTIN: And you're going to do it?

CLAUDIA: Yes, but I don't want the money.

MARTIN: You're crazy.

CLAUDIA: Okay, I'm crazy.

MARTIN: You'd let yourself be inseminated with *his* sperm?

CLAUDIA: He doesn't do it personally. You use a syringe.

MARTIN: But *his* sperm? Come on.

CLAUDIA: He *is* married to my sister.

MARTIN: In her case, love was *very* blind. Doesn't he understand what pregnancy puts you through? My sister's pregnant and she looks like a blimp, waddles like a duck, had three months of chucking up every morning, and there's the whole bloody birth thing. Said to be like rooting a pumpkin.

CLAUDIA: Please.

MARTIN: It's got risks. Big risks. What was I supposed to do to make sure it was his? Wear a condom? Or have the kind of sex you haven't wished to contemplate up to now?

CLAUDIA: As well as paying very generously for me to have a year off, he was going to send you to New York for three months.

MARTIN: What?

CLAUDIA: He said he thought of the condoms but this was more certain.

MARTIN: I can't believe this.

CLAUDIA: He did his research. He knows how desperately you want to check out the art scene over there.

There's a pause.

MARTIN: If you *are* determined to do something as gruesome as this you *deserve* the money.

CLAUDIA: Martin!

MARTIN: You've been wracking your brains trying to work out how you can take a year off to do a Master's degree.

CLAUDIA: I'm doing this for Helen. Not to advance my career.

MARTIN: Three months in New York? All expenses paid?

CLAUDIA: Martin, I'm not taking his money.

MARTIN: Him wanking off down the hallway while you've got your legs in the air waiting. Jesus. You *should* be paid.

CLAUDIA: I'm doing it to help Helen.

MARTIN: Why shouldn't we get some of that prick's money. He's a dead-set capo bastard who's lied and cheated his way to a fucking fortune.

CLAUDIA: No Martin! [*Pause.*] No.

>   *They sit there.*

SCENE FIVE

City café. Two weeks later.

CLAUDIA *waits impatiently. Her mother,* MARGARET, *52, arrives.*

CLAUDIA: Hi Mum.

MARGARET: Sorry. Always late. But this time it's for a good reason. We look as if we're going to win the case.

CLAUDIA: Which case?

MARGARET: Claudia, do you *ever* listen to me?

CLAUDIA: Sorry, I've been a bit preoccupied lately.

MARGARET: Traditional aboriginal designs being ripped off and reproduced on mugs and tea-towels and stuff. I think the ruling is going to go in our favour.

CLAUDIA: Good.

MARGARET: It's going to mean a lot to our aboriginal people. In self respect, in royalties, and even more important than that, it'll be a huge symbolic victory.

CLAUDIA: Good.

MARGARET: White Australia won't be able to ignore any longer the fact that our predecessors had an intricate spiritual culture in many ways superior to our own.

CLAUDIA: Good.

MARGARET: It *is* more important than just designs on tea-towels.

CLAUDIA: Mum, we're here today to talk about other things?

MARGARET: Sorry, but you asked me what I was doing and I told you.

CLAUDIA: I didn't ask, actually.

MARGARET: Sometimes the work I'm doing *is* important enough to warrant a sentence or two.

CLAUDIA: It always has been.

ACT ONE

MARGARET: I won't ever mention it again. You said you wanted to talk.
CLAUDIA: This pregnancy thing.
MARGARET: It was never a brilliant idea in my book.
CLAUDIA: So you made clear. And you were right. I can't go through with it.
MARGARET: It's a bit late now, isn't it? Helen and Mark are over the moon.
CLAUDIA: I've been reading up on what pregnancy does to your body. And every labour I've heard about in the last month has lasted thirty-six hours.
MARGARET: Might've been an idea to do your research before you said yes.
CLAUDIA: I felt I had to offer!
MARGARET: Why?
CLAUDIA: [*incredulous*] Why? Because Helen was devastated.
MARGARET: Your impulse to help was laudable but it was never very realistic.
CLAUDIA: No. My emotions took over. Sorry. Terrible crime.
MARGARET: Well, it wasn't, was it?
CLAUDIA: When we were kids Helen and I were very, very close.
MARGARET: No more than any other sisters.
CLAUDIA: Yes, a lot more. You weren't there all that often.

MARGARET senses where this is heading and wants to avoid it.

MARGARET: Is the health thing the *only* reason you want to back out?
CLAUDIA: As soon as I swell up, Martin will run.
MARGARET: Frankly, good riddance.
CLAUDIA: Mum!
MARGARET: All men are self-obsessed but Martin thinks he's the only pickle that was ever put in a jar.
CLAUDIA: You have been known to be a little self-absorbed yourself.
MARGARET: Women have to be or they spend their whole life mopping up other people's problems.
CLAUDIA: No one could ever accuse you of being a mopper.
MARGARET: Don't you be one either. This is Helen's problem. You should've kept right away, but unfortunately you didn't. You played the heroine, got the kudos, and it'd be very cruel to back out now.
CLAUDIA: I thought you might've been a *tiny* bit more understanding.

MARGARET: You said the chances of the procedure working are only one in five.

CLAUDIA: The first attempt.

MARGARET: Do one and say that's enough.

CLAUDIA: I can't.

MARGARET: Then go and tell your sister and don't prolong everyone's agony any longer. She's shopping for baby clothes already.

CLAUDIA: Oh Jesus.

MARGARET: And if you do get pregnant, for God's sake take his money and get yourself something out of it.

CLAUDIA: I will be getting something out of it. Like giving someone something they'd never be able to have?

MARGARET: Do you want men trampling you all your life because you never bothered to get a Master's degree?

> MARGARET *looks at her daughter.* CLAUDIA *holds the gaze, then looks away.*

SCENE SIX

The Prince of Wales Hospital. Ten months later.

CLAUDIA *is sitting up in a hospital bed.* HELEN *and* MARK *and* MARTIN *are around the bed.* HELEN *is holding the baby and she and* MARK *are euphoric.*

HELEN: It's so unfair. She looks just like Mark. Not the slightest bit of our side of the family.

MARK: She doesn't look like anyone. Babies never do.

HELEN: [*to* MARK] I can see your nose. Your eyes. Claudie, you have a hold.

> *She holds the baby out to* CLAUDIA. CLAUDIA *shakes her head.*

CLAUDIA: You keep her. She's yours.

HELEN: She's both ours. As far as I'm concerned she'll always have two mothers.

ACT ONE

HELEN *holds the baby out to* CLAUDIA, *but* CLAUDIA *is reluctant to take it.*

MARK: Don't force her, love. They did say it's best if you do most of the handling.

HELEN: It doesn't mean she can't hold it, Mark.

CLAUDIA: I did this for you guys.

MARK: And we're never going to forget, believe me.

HELEN *hands the baby to* MARK *and hugs her sister with great passion.*

HELEN: We're certainly not.

She takes the baby back.

It was just so amazingly generous of you.

CLAUDIA: I did manage to get a Master's degree out of it. If they pass that final assignment.

HELEN: I think it's brilliant you managed to keep studying right to the end.

CLAUDIA: It was touch and go. By eight months my brain was yoghurt.

MARK: From what I've heard it should really make a difference to your career.

CLAUDIA: [*nodding*] Two other firms have put out feelers already.

MARK: That's great.

HELEN: Claudie, you've made us just so happy.

CLAUDIA: I'm so glad. For both of you.

HELEN: It's just such an amazing thing to do. You *are* fine about us having it?

CLAUDIA: Of course!

HELEN: You did all the work and I couldn't take it if I felt—

MARK: Helen, we've discussed all this and I've paid a lot of money.

HELEN: Mark, the money is not the issue.

MARK: And the baby isn't just Claudia's. It's half mine.

CLAUDIA: Please, both of you. The last thing I could cope with now is a baby. I'll sign the adoption papers as soon as they'll let me.

HELEN: You're absolutely sure?

CLAUDIA: Katrina is well and truly yours.

MARTIN: Absolutely. It was bad enough living with your daughter when she was still inside.

MARK: Thanks for that. It couldn't've been fun.

MARTIN: Frankly it was hellish. My life with a whale.

HELEN: Oh, she's not Katrina anymore, we're calling her Kelly.

CLAUDIA: [*looking at* MARTIN] Kelly?

HELEN: You don't like it?

CLAUDIA: Not as much as Katrina.

HELEN: Mark really likes Kelly.

MARK: It's a lively, fun-type name. Katrina's a tad pretentious.

MARTIN: I'd think twice about Kelly.

MARK: [*defensively*] Why?

MARTIN: Call 'Kelly' and every kid within two miles'll yell 'Yes Dad'.

MARK: It's not that common.

HELEN: It is, Mark, but if you like it...

MARK: [*defensively*] I like it.

He turns to MARTIN. *The source of irritation.*

Selling more of your stuff these days?

MARTIN: Some.

MARK: Hard to make a living out of painting unless you were a big name I guess?

MARTIN: Being a 'big name' is not really what I'm about.

MARK: So still teaching?

MARTIN: A little.

MARK: You looked into the way you're marketing yourself?

MARTIN: Not really.

MARK: You should. Find your unique point of difference and market the hell out of yourself. Thought you might have picked up on some of that stuff when you were in New York.

MARTIN: I was actually looking at art.

MARK: Picasso was a shameless self-publicist.

MARTIN: Exactly.

MARK: Mind you he also had talent.

HELEN: [*sensing the vibes are getting a little tricky*] Mark, it's time to take Kelly back to the nursery. You're sure you don't want a hold, Claudie?

CLAUDIA: No, I'm fine.

HELEN: [*kissing her*] This is the happiest day of my life. We'll tell her at the appropriate time who her real mother is, of course.

MARK: I've got real reservations about that.

HELEN: We don't have to talk about it now. The wonderful thing is that she's here.

> HELEN *and* MARK *leave with the baby,* MARK *nodding awkward goodbyes to* CLAUDIA *and* MARTIN *as he goes.*

MARTIN: There's the answer. Find my unique point of difference. Whip off an ear like Van Gogh.

CLAUDIA: Most artists do put in *some* effort promoting themselves.

MARTIN: Sorry. I'm not about to go sucking up to anyone. If dealers prefer fashionable crap to genuine innovation then that's their problem, not mine.

CLAUDIA: You keep telling me how much you hate teaching. I just don't want to see you stuck with it forever.

MARTIN: Don't worry. I won't be. You okay?

CLAUDIA: Apart from being totally exhausted. Yeah.

MARTIN: I mean about giving up the kid?

CLAUDIA: You still terrified I'll bond with it and ruin your life?

MARTIN: You must have felt something for it after all that work.

CLAUDIA: Yeah. The hormone thing kicks in pretty hard.

MARTIN: It is going to be all right?

CLAUDIA: [*nodding*] As long as I don't start cuddling it. Now she's called Kelly it's going to be easier.

> MARTIN *smiles and embraces her.*

MARTIN: You did a great thing for those two. I just hope they appreciate it.

SCENE SEVEN

City café: 1985.

Again CLAUDIA *waits for her mother who hurries in and sits.*

MARGARET: Sorry. Things are frantic.

CLAUDIA: I'm very busy too. Landmark case?

MARGARET: Crucial. A European beer manufacturer stole the name and marketing campaign of a local firm.

CLAUDIA: Big stuff.

MARGARET: Hugely important principles of law.

CLAUDIA: Of course.

MARGARET: If we win we'll be sending a message. Just because we're on the other side of the world doesn't mean our intellectual property is any less sacrosanct.

CLAUDIA: Especially a home-grown beer. I'm actually working on something quite substantial myself.

MARGARET: Good.

CLAUDIA: A big merger. Dotting Is and crossing Ts and guarding against every eventuality.

MARGARET: Yes, commercial law can be tedious.

CLAUDIA: I *like* tying up loose ends.

MARGARET: I believe you've been speaking to your father?

CLAUDIA: I've had coffee with him once or twice. Since he saw me in the hospital he seems to want to re-establish contact.

MARGARET: Guilt.

CLAUDIA: It's all very much arm's length. Don't worry.

MARGARET: Why would I worry?

CLAUDIA: You didn't like it when Helen started seeing him.

MARGARET: It's just so easy for him to be charming now.

CLAUDIA: I probably should have seen him too.

MARGARET: I didn't stop you.

CLAUDIA: I stayed away out of loyalty to you.

MARGARET: Just remember that he was sleeping with Tanya when I was pregnant with you. And she was just the last of a long line.

CLAUDIA: Mum, I'm not about to reclaim him.

MARGARET: I know your sister bad mouths me to him.

CLAUDIA: Well, I wouldn't know and frankly I'm not interested.

MARGARET: If you had've seen him back then. Australia's only tenured beatnik. Telling his students to break out of suburban conformity, which was code for: 'Have sex with everyone. Especially me.' Are you well? Everything fine?

CLAUDIA: [*defensively*] Yes.

MARGARET: How's Martin?

CLAUDIA: Fine.

MARGARET: I wish that self-absorption had some talent to justify it.

CLAUDIA: Mum, he's still in his twenties.

MARGARET: He's sold three or four paintings in his life. And when you look at them you know why. You're going to end up supporting him.

CLAUDIA: He's a terrific artist and he'll eventually sell heaps.

Maria Theodorakis (left) as Claudia and Deidre Rubenstein as Margaret in the 2003 Melbourne Theatre Company production. (Photo: Jeff Busby)

MARGARET: Hmm.

CLAUDIA: I'm happier with him than any of the others. By miles.

MARGARET: Why?

CLAUDIA: He's highly intelligent, witty, ironic, radical and we're very… [*embarrassed*] compatible. Physically.

MARGARET: For God's sake, don't let *that* ever sway you. The best lover I ever had was a Japanese vibrator. Helen says you're seeing quite a lot of little Kelly.

CLAUDIA: I like to keep in touch. Helen appreciates it.

> MARGARET *looks a little dubious.*

Doesn't she?

> MARGARET *says nothing.*

She doesn't?

MARGARET: I'm sure she does. I think you've just got to be careful.

CLAUDIA: About what?

MARGARET: It's hard for people to cope with a debt they can never really repay.

CLAUDIA: What's she said?

MARGARET: [*lying*] She hasn't said anything. I've just got a feeling that…

CLAUDIA: What?

MARGARET: You probably shouldn't crowd them.

CLAUDIA: I'm not. I never want to be anything more than a good aunt.

> MARGARET *looks at her and nods.*

SCENE EIGHT

Claudia and Martin's flat. 1990.

Late night. MARTIN, *who is working on a drawing board, looks up as* CLAUDIA *comes in. She looks energised and happy.*

MARTIN: How did it go?

CLAUDIA: She was a little monster. An absolute little monster.

MARTIN: Again?

CLAUDIA: She's getting worse. Rude, interrupts, demands things as if they're her perfect right, corrects everything you say.

She shakes her head in mock despair.

MARTIN: How'd she like the show?

CLAUDIA: Spent her whole time criticising holes in the plot. Loudly. 'Why is Madame Butterfly so sad?' Because Pinkerton left her. 'She should be glad. He's fat as a pig.' Then when Madame B killed herself she got very scathing about the red ribbons. Told everyone within earshot that they didn't look anything like blood.

MARTIN: She's going to be a critic.

CLAUDIA: Or a lawyer. She's as funny as hell, but I'm really starting to get concerned. Her temper tantrums are just appalling. Still. And she's nearly six. Helen and Mark just give in and give her exactly what she wants.

MARTIN *peels off a sheet of paper and shows her.*

MARTIN: What do you think?

CLAUDIA *chuckles.*

CLAUDIA: Keating's not going to be happy.

MARTIN: What right have they got to call themselves a Labor party? They're hand in hand with big business keeping workers' wages down.

CLAUDIA: I just hope our Treasurer doesn't scream down the phone at your editor again.

MARTIN: [*shrugging*] I'm only a cartoonist by accident. If they want to get rid of me I'll go back to my real work.

CLAUDIA: I'm really worried about that girl.

MARTIN: She's got two parents. Don't obsess about her.

CLAUDIA: She's spoilt rotten. Mark buys her everything she asks for to make up for the fact he's never there. What she needs more than anything is a damn good smack, and sometimes I'm pretty close to giving her one.

MARTIN: Do it.

CLAUDIA: The schedule they've got her on would make your average CEO seem bone lazy. French classes Tuesday, violin Wednesday, Music and Movement Friday, and on the weekends there's jazz ballet, swimming and ET.

MARTIN: ET?

CLAUDIA: Empathy training.

MARTIN: How the fuck do you teach empathy? 'Okay, little ones. I'd like you to point to someone *much* more miserable than you are and share their pain.'

CLAUDIA: They're trying to turn her into a superchild. It's insane. She'll either become totally unbearable or burn out.

SCENE NINE

Eastern Suburbs bistro. 1996.

HELEN *waits for her mother.* MARGARET, *as always, is late. And* HELEN *looks up as she comes towards her.*

MARGARET: Sorry. Sorry. How are you?

HELEN: Fine.

MARGARET: Where's Mark right now?

HELEN: Hong Kong. Then London. Then Chicago.

MARGARET: He's never home.

HELEN: All he does is stomp round the house and shout into the phone when he is. Apparently in order to make money you have to be in a perpetual state of rage.

MARGARET: I worry about you.

HELEN: I know you can't stand Mark, but he works hard and we live well.

MARGARET: I've never said I can't stand him.

HELEN: You don't have to. Whenever he's in the room your lip curls.

MARGARET: He's just so *incredibly* boastful, Helen. We all know how successful he is. Does he have to broadcast it quite so often?

HELEN: For someone who left school at fifteen he's done incredibly well. And if someone in the family occasionally acknowledged that, he wouldn't feel so looked down on.

MARGARET: Looked down on? You live in one of the most luxurious houses in Sydney.

HELEN: It wouldn't matter if we lived in a palace. You'd still all sneer.

MARGARET: No one sneers.

HELEN: You do. Because we don't share the trendy views the rest of this family find obligatory.

MARGARET: What trendy views?

HELEN: The republic and multiculturalism. And pouring taxpayers' money into aboriginals, the arts and the unemployed. This country gives everyone a fair chance and if they haven't got the drive or the brains to utilise it, that's their fault.

MARGARET: I think it's more complex than that.

HELEN: Mum, I didn't come here to get a lecture.

MARGARET: You seem to be lecturing me.

HELEN: Will you just tell Claudia to stop carrying on as if she's got some kind of proprietorial claim on Kelly.

MARGARET: She's just acting like any aunt would.

HELEN: Rubbish. She rings her every second night and takes her out every weekend. Movies, shows, cafés. Spoils her rotten. And then she comes home and says Aunty Claudie lets me do this, Auntie Claudie lets me do that.

MARGARET: Kelly's just playing you off against each other.

HELEN: Yes, well it's got to stop. I'm grateful for what she did for us, but she seems to think she's got some kind of claim.

MARGARET: I'm sure she doesn't.

HELEN: Mother, she does. She's trying to take her over and it's getting me angry and depressed. And you can tell her that.

MARGARET: Helen, it's up to you to tell her yourself.

HELEN: I'd lose my temper. I'd get too angry.

MARGARET: Well, I'm not doing it for you.

HELEN: No, of course.

MARGARET: What's that meant to mean?

HELEN: Mum, when could I ever count on you for any backup. Until I was about four I thought poor old Beryl was my mother. You were just some person who stuck your head in the door a few seconds before I went to sleep.

MARGARET: They were tough years for me.

HELEN: And for me.

MARGARET: I was a woman in the legal profession trying to establish a career. It was a total boys club in those days.

HELEN: The only one in the school play whose mother didn't come to see her.

MARGARET: For God's sake, Helen, you were only playing the cat.

HELEN: I cried for hours.

MARGARET: I'm sorry. I'm sure you were a very fine cat, and if there's one part of my life I could re-run I'd be there seeing you be a very fine cat, but this is the two hundredth cat absence mention, and I think it's enough!

HELEN: It hurt.

MARGARET: Point taken!

There's a silence.

HELEN: Mark's getting very upset too.

MARGARET: At what?

HELEN: Kelly came home from one of her 'outings' with her aunt and asked us why we haven't got our own flag. Mark was really angry.

MARGARET: It's a good question.

HELEN: We've got our own flag. Our soldiers have fought and died under it.

MARGARET: It's still got England's flag in the corner.

HELEN: England's part of our history. England gave us democracy.

MARGARET: Good, but it's high time we had our own head of state, not vowel-strangled Betty Windsor and her appalling brood.

HELEN: See? Sneers. You won't speak to Claudia, will you?

MARGARET: Helen, if you've got a problem with her, you speak to her.

HELEN: If it was Claudia asking for help it'd be a different story.

MARGARET: Helen, that's nonsense.

HELEN: I've never been forgiven for discovering that Dad's not a piece of bottom-feeding bacterial sludge, have I?

MARGARET: He did leave me when I was pregnant with Claudia.

HELEN: You told him to go.

MARGARET: That was shocking of me. All he was doing was sleeping with one of his students.

HELEN: Maybe if you'd been more…

MARGARET: What?

HELEN: Interested? Obliging?

MARGARET: Is that what he's told you?

HELEN: I'm not always in the mood, but for God's sake, if it keeps them happy for the rest of the week, then what the hell.

MARGARET: The only reason I didn't have more frequent sex with your father was that he was usually doing it with someone else! What other rubbish has he told you?

HELEN: Nothing.

MARGARET: That I'm obsessive? Driven?

HELEN: You are.

MARGARET: In a man it's called 'focused' and 'determined'.

HELEN: You aren't a man. You're a *woman*. And you were supposed to be a *mother*.

MARGARET: As a mother, however flawed, am I allowed to voice some concerns about you?

HELEN: What?

MARGARET: You're wasting your potential.

HELEN: I'm 'just' a wife, and 'just' a mother?

MARGARET: If anything you were brighter than Claudia.

HELEN: And now she works an eighty-hour week and is incredibly happy, except there's no time to have a child, so she tries to steal mine.

MARGARET: Helen, she sees her one or two hours a week.

HELEN: Maximum damage in minimum time. We've already got a *huge* discipline problem at school. Did you know that?

MARGARET: She's a spirited young girl.

HELEN: She got up at assembly and asked the headmistress why there were no aboriginal girls at the school.

MARGARET: [*laughing*] And the headmistress said they were perfectly free to apply.

HELEN: You hear everything, don't you?

MARGARET: They are. As long as their parents have twenty thousand per kid per year.

HELEN: I'm sorry, but I don't want Kelly becoming one of those awful people who take great delight in criticising people who make something of their lives.

MARGARET: Helen, relax.

HELEN: I do twenty times as much for her as Claudia, and it's as if I don't exist.

MARGARET: It's called having an adolescent girl.

HELEN: I'd like some acknowledgment.

MARGARET: She takes you for granted. Don't do so much. You're a twenty-four-hour shuttle service for that girl.

HELEN: It's not like the days when you packed us off on a bus when I was barely six.

MARGARET: There's a train that goes right to her school a few minutes away.

HELEN: Those trains are packed with boys from all kinds of schools.

MARGARET: She's got to learn to cope. Get on with your own life.

HELEN: I am. But somehow everything I do doesn't count. I'm organising the whole renovation and redecoration of the upstairs guestrooms, in case you hadn't noticed. And then comes the kitchen.

MARGARET: Helen, your kitchen is the best kitchen I've ever seen. Why on *earth* would you want to renovate it?

HELEN: I'm sick of being stuck behind a marble barrier while everyone else enjoys themselves. It's not ergonomically designed for communicative flow.

    MARGARET *sighs*.

[*Irritated*] Tell me exactly what I am supposed to be doing with my life!

MARGARET: Using your brain. You used to have a good one. Until you started partying your life away.

HELEN: Mother, I know you'll never understand, but university was *torture* for me. Philosophy. Pedantic hair-splitting hell. Psychology. The human mind? Forget it. Applied statistics.

MARGARET: History. You loved it.

HELEN: It was marginally more bearable than the rest.

MARGARET: I'm sure you'd find it more interesting now.

HELEN: No thanks. All my friends who've gone back to study are just so *tedious*. [*Imitating them*] 'Oh Migod, I have to *race* to the library. I got A-plus for my last assignment, but this one's going to be a *disaster.*' There's only one explanation why someone as dumb as Marion Christie is getting A-pluses. The same way she got everything else in her life.

MARGARET: I really think you'd like it.

HELEN: Mum, all I want to be is a good mother. And it would help one hell of a lot if my sister wasn't trying to take over.

She looks at MARGARET. *Message clear.*

SCENE TEN

City café. A week later.

MARGARET *waits for her daughter, looking at her watch and sighing.*
CLAUDIA *appears.* CLAUDIA *is triumphant.*

CLAUDIA: Sorry.

MARGARET: That's fine.

CLAUDIA: Richard hauled me into his office just as I was on the way out.

MARGARET: And?

CLAUDIA: A senior partner. Finally. Can you believe it?

MARGARET: You've worked hard enough.

CLAUDIA: They tried everything they could to stop me, but my billings were so good last year that they had no option.

MARGARET: Congratulations. You're about the same age as I was.

CLAUDIA: Actually three years younger. But who's counting.

MARGARET: You are obviously.

CLAUDIA: You're the yardstick, aren't you?

MARGARET: It was harder in my day you know.

CLAUDIA: [*tersely*] You couldn't let me have a little credit. Just once?

MARGARET: I did, dear. I said congratulations and I meant it.

CLAUDIA: So, how's retirement?

MARGARET: Retirement? What a joke. They've made me chair of the body corporate, and I've been plonked on the board of about four different charities and three arts organisations.

CLAUDIA: You could have said no.

MARGARET: Community service is still an important concept to my generation.

CLAUDIA: You said you wanted to talk about Helen?

MARGARET: I took her to lunch and a whole lifetime's resentment came pouring out. What a rotten mother I'd been. How her father is all sweetness and light.

CLAUDIA: She's a drama queen. Don't let it get to you.

MARGARET: Was I really *that* preoccupied with my work?

CLAUDIA: Yes, but hey, we survived.

MARGARET: You feel resentful too?

CLAUDIA: It's worse for Helen. She's got this thing that I was the favourite.

MARGARET: She was such a *demanding* little beast. The truth is that I loved going to work so I could leave her with Beryl and get the hell out of there.

 CLAUDIA *smiles.*

No one ever prepared me for parenthood. A gaping little mouth that's either sucking or emitting the most God-awful scream. If I'd had any inkling I would have never let it happen.

CLAUDIA: There go Helen and I.

MARGARET: It did happen and I got to love you both dearly. You don't seriously think otherwise?

CLAUDIA: There have been moments of doubt.

MARGARET: In Helen's case, total doubt. [*She sighs.*] Being a grandparent is so much easier. Swan in, shower them with sugar bombs and presents, a few hugs, then out again.

CLAUDIA: That's why I like being an aunt.

 MARGARET *looks away.*

What? Helen's been whining again? For God's sake, once a fortnight I take Kelly to a movie or something.

MARGARET: She says once a week. And you ring every second night.

CLAUDIA: Kelly rings *me*. *What* is going on in that woman's head?

MARGARET: She's jealous.

CLAUDIA: That is *ludicrous*.

 MARGARET *remains silent.*

Don't you think?

MARGARET: Kelly does seem to relate to you very strongly.

CLAUDIA: I'm giving her another viewpoint on life.

MARGARET: Maybe it's a tad precocious for a twelve-year-old to be putting the Palestinian case to her Jewish teacher.

CLAUDIA: Are you saying the Palestinians haven't got a case?

MARGARET: Claudia, you're not just an aunt. Helen is terrified Kelly will find out the truth.

CLAUDIA: If you want my opinion, she should've been told long ago. Then it wouldn't have become a big deal.

MARGARET: I don't think your sister could face it right now.

CLAUDIA: I've no earthly intention of trying to displace Helen. She's done the mothering. She's the mother.

MARGARET: It's not as simple as that in her mind, believe me.

CLAUDIA: Simple honesty would have solved all this years ago.

MARGARET *sighs and shrugs.*

SCENE ELEVEN

Claudia's place. That evening.

CLAUDIA *enters fuming as* MARTIN *works away at one of his cartoons.*

CLAUDIA: My sister's bitching to Mum about me stealing her daughter's affections.

MARTIN: Well, aren't you?

    CLAUDIA *stares at him.*

You gave them Kelly which was a wonderful thing to do, but I have to be honest. There are times I think you're trying to grab her back.

CLAUDIA: Martin, I'm not!

MARTIN: You're obsessed with her. There are other things happening in the world.

    CLAUDIA *stares at him, taken aback by the anger and distress in his voice.*

CLAUDIA: What's wrong?

MARTIN: What would you care?

CLAUDIA: What's wrong?

MARTIN: Fred knocked back my cartoon.

CLAUDIA: Keating as Suharto's puppet? It's great.

MARTIN: Fred said he won't run any more attacks on Keating. Thinks he's our greatest Prime Minister since Menzies. Opened our economy to the world and made our slackarse unions feel the heat.

CLAUDIA: I can't believe it.

MARTIN: Keating signs a secret military deal with the world's most corrupt leader, brokered by the CIA no doubt, and it's 'off limits' for comment.

CLAUDIA: I can't believe it.

MARTIN: It's not enough that we've been training Indonesia's East Timor torture squads, now we're sharing our military secrets with them. And I've also been told to lay off John Howard.

CLAUDIA: You're joking.

MARTIN: They know he's going to win the election and they don't want to lose favour. They're pushing me to the point I'll have to resign.

CLAUDIA: There'd be a huge outcry.

MARTIN: From who?

CLAUDIA: You're the top political cartoonist in the country. Look at the letters you get.

MARTIN: I've had two in the last month. One said I was a traitor to the white race and the other was full of excrement.

CLAUDIA: You rouse strong feelings.

MARTIN: Indeed, as I found out when Fred shoved the last readership survey under my nose.

CLAUDIA: You wouldn't be doing your job if *some* people didn't hate your work.

MARTIN: It seems that I'm doing my job brilliantly then. I'm hated by just about everyone. Too dark, too bitter, too obscure, and too cruel. And obsessed by far-left conspiracy theories.

CLAUDIA: Maybe the conspiracy thing's partly true, but / everyone I know—

MARTIN: [*overlapping*] You really think the Oklahoma bombing was just the work of a couple of mad right-wingers? It had CIA stamped all over it.

CLAUDIA: Okay. Fine.
MARTIN: Who benefits from the bombing? Legislation rushed through to give total surveillance powers to the FBI and the CIA. It's the end of any real dissent about *anything* over there. The left is the *real* target.
CLAUDIA: Martin, if you'd let me finish, I was trying to say that everyone I know thinks your work is brilliant.
MARTIN: The people we know are a tiny left elite.
CLAUDIA: That doesn't mean what we believe in is wrong.
MARTIN: No. It just makes it hard to stay employed.

SCENE TWELVE

Helen's house. Some months later.

MARK *and* HELEN *enter the living room of their house.* MARK *is in a bad mood.*

MARK: Why did you have to invite them back for drinks?
HELEN: So they could drive my mother home.
MARK: I would have done it.
HELEN: [*looking around and keeping her voice down*] You always complain so much when you do.
MARK: Why can't we get her a taxi?

     MARGARET *appears.*

MARGARET: How was your evening?
MARK: Food's really gone off at Lucio's. Not going there again.
HELEN: Those marble floors. Such a din. Can't hear a word people say.
MARK: That was the good part. All those two ever say is left-wing garbage.
HELEN: They're coming in for a drink, Mum. Just parking their car.
MARK: They'll drive you home. Is Kelly asleep?
MARGARET: Fast asleep.
MARK: Give you any trouble?
MARGARET: None at all. She's such a funny girl. We spent most of the night laughing.

MARK: She should've been doing her homework.

MARGARET: She had that done in a flash. [*To* HELEN] So it was a good evening? Apart from the noise level?

HELEN: [*looking at* MARK] I know you keep pushing us to do this Mum, but really we've got very little in common.

MARK: Nothing at all.

MARGARET: Did you talk about…?

HELEN: No.

MARGARET: I did raise it with your sister.

HELEN: It hasn't stopped her chattering on to Kelly on the phone every second night.

MARGARET: Kelly rings Claudia a lot of the time.

HELEN: There are ways of discouraging that.

> CLAUDIA *and* MARTIN *enter and greet* MARGARET.

CLAUDIA: Hi Mum.

MARK: What'll it be?

MARTIN: We can't stay long. Mineral water. I'm driving.

CLAUDIA: Brandy. I'm not. So how was Kelly, Mum?

HELEN: Doesn't sound like much homework was done.

> MARK *pours two brandies, one of which he hands to* CLAUDIA *and the other he tosses down himself.* HELEN *pours herself and* MARTIN *a mineral water.*

MARGARET: [*to* CLAUDIA] We did chatter on a bit. She's so funny.

HELEN: Not when I'm around.

MARGARET: One of her school friend's brothers fancies her and she's giving him a hard time.

CLAUDIA: [*laughing*] She told me.

HELEN: A thirteen-year-old shouldn't be encouraged to think about boys.

MARGARET: The boy's thinking of her, I'm afraid.

CLAUDIA: And she's handling it pretty well.

> MARK *pours himself another large brandy and tosses half of that down as well. He picks up a large, glossy brochure that has been conveniently placed on a mantelpiece nearby.*

ACT ONE

MARK: [*to* MARTIN] Here's the prospectus for our new venture I was telling you about.

    MARTIN *takes it, opens it and nods.*

Oversubscribed three days after we sent it out. Three new five-star hotels with championship courses. That's the one in Vanuatu, that's New Caledonia and that's Fiji. All the courses Greg Norman designed. Never played golf?

MARTIN: No.

MARK: Pity. I could get you into any of these resorts at half price.

MARTIN: Even half price will be stretching my new budget.

MARGARET: Sorry to hear that you resigned, Martin.

MARTIN: They were trying to censor me.

MARK: [*indicating the prospectus*] If you're looking for a good living there's a fortune to be made out of the design of these things.

MARTIN: You'd be better off with a graphic designer.

MARK: [*tossing down the rest of the brandy and pouring himself another*] What are you going to do then?

MARTIN: Syndicate of investors wants me to start my own magazine. This country desperately needs a radical voice.

CLAUDIA: Martin's cartoons connect with a whole heap of people.

MARK: I have to be honest. I never met anyone who liked them.

HELEN: A lot of people I know felt that the way you treated John Howard was really offensive.

CLAUDIA: Helen. His election is a disaster.

MARK: The voters happen to disagree with you. It's called democracy.

CLAUDIA: John Howard is a creepy throwback to an Australian that doesn't exist anymore.

MARK: Strange he was voted in.

MARTIN: The electorate were saturated with far-right propaganda.

MARK: Paid for by the CIA no doubt?

MARTIN: [*nodding*] Three point eight million of it.

MARK: Says who?

MARTIN: We're a key South-East Asian surveillance facility. And their whole nuclear war control strategy depends on Pine Gap.

MARK: That's rubbish. We're an independent, fully-functioning, transparent democracy and I'm proud to be a citizen.

MARTIN: Democracy? Don't make me laugh.

MARK: What are we? Do tell.

MARTIN: A country in which a tiny, super-rich elite rigs everything in their own favour. The wealthiest man in the country pays no bloody taxes! And boasts about it.

MARK: We live in a country which allowed me the freedom to do something with my life. I'm proud to live here, and I'm proud of what I've achieved.

MARTIN: What exactly is you *have* achieved, Mark old son?

CLAUDIA: Martin.

MARTIN: No, bugger it. He bribes the leaders of third-world countries to let him build ecologically disastrous golf resorts—

MARK: Bribe?

CLAUDIA: Induce.

MARTIN: And those resorts are used by a tiny super-affluent elite, and none of their money ever gets back to the islanders.

MARK: We provide something other people are prepared to pay for. The world's tried socialism. It doesn't work.

MARTIN: You made two million dollars last year I'm told.

HELEN: Mum, that was told to you in *confidence*!

MARTIN: [*to* MARK] Frankly, that's obscene.

CLAUDIA: Martin.

MARK: [*angrily*] Mate, this is a tough world and I've worked like a dog and earned every cent of it. If you can't hold your job that's your fault.

MARTIN: I resigned!

MARK: And just for your information John Howard is going to be our greatest Prime Minister ever!

HELEN: We won't have millions upon millions of taxpayers' money being wasted on dole bludgers and the multicultural industry.

MARK: If people come here they should learn our language and forget their old hatreds. What do you want Australia to be? Another Yugoslavia.

MARTIN: Forget tolerance, forget diversity.

MARK: Diversity. Diversity. You know what? I *loathe* that word. I bloody near vomit every time I hear it. You want to know why John Howard was voted in on a landslide. Because the people out there hate it too. They hate people like you trying to change the Australia they know and love without so much as asking their opinion.

HELEN: This is the best country in the world and I wish you'd stop telling Kelly that it isn't.

CLAUDIA: Okay, Australia's perfect, the whole world's perfect.

HELEN: A thirteen-year-old shouldn't be forced to take the world's problems on her shoulders.

MARGARET: Helen, I don't think what Claudia's telling her is doing any damage.

HELEN: You wouldn't. You've always been on her side. But what the both of you seem to have forgotten is that Kelly is my child, and I'd like her to have my values.

CLAUDIA: Of course she's your child.

HELEN: Sometimes I'm not sure you accept that.

MARK: Even though I paid a bloody fortune for you to have a year off!

CLAUDIA: Of course I accept it. But I *do* have feelings for her.

MARK: That doesn't entitle you to take her over.

CLAUDIA: Half of this paranoia is because you haven't even told her the truth.

MARK: Keep your voice down.

HELEN: You more than half own her now. What do you want, to destroy me?

CLAUDIA: Don't be such a bloody drama queen. She knows damn well who her mother is.

HELEN: It certainly doesn't feel like that to me.

MARTIN: The longer you put off telling her, the worse it's going to be.

MARK: This's got *nothing* to do with you, mate. You got three bloody months in New York!

HELEN: [*to* CLAUDIA] Why doesn't she just move in with you and be done with it.

CLAUDIA: Helen, that's the last thing I want.

MARK: No, you just want us to feed, clothe, educate and care for her so you can swan in and play fairy godmother.

HELEN: She even looks like you. People remark on it. Do you know that? Can you try and see it from my point of view. She is my child. I love her. I brought her up. And you come in and make yourself her heroine. [*Suddenly very angry*] If you want a daughter then bloody well go and have one of your own. Don't try and steal mine! Don't bloody well try and steal mine!

> HELEN *starts to cry.* MARK *comforts her, looking over her shoulder at the other three with angry intensity.* CLAUDIA *moves towards her sister, but* MARK *turns on her angrily.*

MARK: Could you both just piss off? You've done enough damage for one night.

> MARK *leaves* HELEN *and advances on all of them.*

Will you all just *go!*

END OF ACT ONE

ACT TWO

SCENE ONE

Claudia's apartment. Later that night.

MARTIN *is pacing up and down angrily.* CLAUDIA, *half undressed, is sitting on a sofa.*

MARTIN: That self-righteous arsehole. He couldn't care less if the whole rest of the world was in terminal ecological collapse, as long as he had his mansion and his BMWs and his wine cellar and his holiday house and whatever.
CLAUDIA: She's right.
MARTIN: Who's right?
CLAUDIA: It's time to have my own child. I *am* trying to steal hers.

    MARTIN *stares at her.*

MARTIN: Now. When I've just lost my fucking job?
CLAUDIA: Martin, I'm thirty-seven. We've put it off long enough as it is.
MARTIN: Women still have babies in their forties.
CLAUDIA: They're the rare ones. And the lucky ones. Read the stats. From where I am now the chances of pregnancy plummet and the chances of birth defects soar.
MARTIN: It's just not a great time for me.
CLAUDIA: I'm a partner in my law firm, for God's sake. We're not going to starve.
MARTIN: I get to stay home and mind the kid?
CLAUDIA: Would it be so terrible for a little while?
MARTIN: I'm not cut out to be one of those wimpy house husbands who chatters on to the mums at nursery.
CLAUDIA: You could go back to your art for a year or two.
MARTIN: And little sprog's going to sit there quietly watching Daddy be creative?

CLAUDIA: Martin, I'm thirty-seven. Time's almost run out. I want a child.
MARTIN: Claudia, what is this thing about kids? We got together because you loved me. Now I'm not enough. Is that the message?
CLAUDIA: It's not about not loving you. I want a child.
MARTIN: Couldn't we wait just another year?
CLAUDIA: No. It might be too late.
MARTIN: Just a year.
CLAUDIA: No, now.
MARTIN: I know how upset you are about Kelly. I understand. I really do. And there *is* a bit of the paternal thing in me, believe it or not. It's just not a great time.
CLAUDIA: Martin, if you don't want to father my child I'll find someone who bloody well will.

> MARTIN *stares at her.*

I mean it.

> *And she does.*

♦ ♦ ♦ ♦ ♦

SCENE TWO

Claudia's apartment. 1998. Nearly two years later.

MARGARET *sits reading a magazine. She's patently not impressed. Offstage we hear* CLAUDIA *and* MARTIN *arguing.* MARGARET *listens and raises her eyebrows and sighs.*

CLAUDIA: [*offstage*] Martin, will you stop your bloody emailing and come!
MARTIN: [*offstage*] There's three people who need urgent answers. I'll be there in a minute.
CLAUDIA: [*offstage*] Mum's waiting.
MARTIN: [*offstage, tense, irritated*] I'll be there in a moment!

> CLAUDIA *comes onstage looking harassed and tries to smile at her mother.*

CLAUDIA: He'll be another few minutes.

MARGARET: There's no hurry. I was so thrilled to get your call.
CLAUDIA: I was getting so angry. You finally decide to have a bloody child and it doesn't happen for nearly two years.
MARGARET: It wasn't your fault. Wasn't his sperm count very low.
CLAUDIA: [*her voice lowered*] Yes, so low my doctor thinks I co-opted the plumber.
MARGARET: If he looks like mine, you should've.
CLAUDIA: God, did I have to work for it. Feet in the air for an hour after sex, making Martin wear daggy loose underpants so his scrotum wouldn't overheat.
MARGARET: I'm not sure I need to know this level of detail.
CLAUDIA: I even put an Inca fertility charm on our bedhead.
MARGARET: Inca? Why Inca?
CLAUDIA: A man and woman coupling. Very graphic. Probably did the trick.
MARGARET: I'm so relieved. I think I've been almost as worried as you.

> CLAUDIA *looks away, emotional and teary-eyed. She stands up, embarrassed.* MARGARET *gets up and hugs her.*

CLAUDIA: I'll call the restaurant and say we'll be a little late. [*She takes out her mobile phone and finds a number.*] Since Martin's turned this place into the office for his magazine. Total chaos. [*To the restaurant*] Jacquie, we're going to be just a little late, okay? [*Nodding*] Thanks. 'Bye.

> *She switches off her phone.*

MARGARET: [*indicating the magazine*] Is it selling many copies?
CLAUDIA: [*looking offstage and lowering her voice*] No.
MARGARET: Didn't he have to borrow a lot of money?
CLAUDIA: [*in a lowered voice*] Yes, mostly mine.

> MARGARET*'s expression tells us what she thinks of that, but she decides not to press the subject any further.*

MARGARET: Having one of your own will help get things back to normal with Helen.
CLAUDIA: I don't really care anymore.
MARGARET: I do.

CLAUDIA: When she *ordered* me to stop phoning Kelly, that was *it*.
MARGARET: I got the impression that was more Mark.
CLAUDIA: What's the difference? She supports everything he says or does.
MARGARET: Kelly tells me you still see each other.
CLAUDIA: In secret. She slips into my office on her way home from school and we have ten minutes or so to chat. It's absurd.

    MARTIN *comes onstage.*

MARTIN: Sorry.
MARGARET: Wonderful news.
MARTIN: Yeah. It's out there at last and people are buying it. Oh, you mean the pregnancy. Yeah. Great. What do you think?
MARGARET: I think it's wonderful.
MARTIN: [*pleased*] Yeah, it's pretty punchy, isn't it? Good layout.
MARGARET: Oh, the magazine?

    She picks it up and looks at it.

MARTIN: Oh, the pregnancy. Yeah, it's great. No more thermometers and sex on schedule.
MARGARET: [*looking at the magazine*] Yes, very... punchy. I suspect it's going to put a few noses out of joint.
MARTIN: I certainly hope so. You like the layout?
MARGARET: Yes, very... modern.
MARTIN: Oh shit. That reminds me. Terry wants an answer on next week's cover.

    He starts to move towards the other room.

CLAUDIA: Martin!
MARTIN: When you're editing a magazine, people need answers!
CLAUDIA: Do it later. Your child needs nourishment. Now.

    MARTIN *storms off ahead of them.* CLAUDIA *sighs and follows.*
    MARGARET, *left alone onstage, grimaces. What a pleasant night she's about to have.*

◆ ◆ ◆ ◆ ◆

SCENE THREE

Claudia's apartment. Three weeks later.

CLAUDIA *is sitting looking straight ahead. Suddenly she screams in pain and rage. She picks up a cushion and beats the sofa with it. Tears stream out of her eyes.* MARTIN *comes in looking worried.*

CLAUDIA: He said it was safe. Relax, he said. You're through the first trimester. It's going to happen. Ninety-eight percent safe. You can talk to her. Tell her stories. And I did. Story after story.

She howls with rage.

MARTIN: It's only a miscarriage.

CLAUDIA: Only? Only?

MARTIN: We'll try again.

CLAUDIA: Martin, it was a miracle it happened last time. It's not going to happen again.

There's a silence.

MARTIN: I don't want a sperm donor. If we are going to have a child, I want it to be mine.

CLAUDIA: Martin, I've been trying and trying to have your child.

MARTIN: If I'm going to bring it up, I want it to be mine.

CLAUDIA: I totally agree. I've always totally agreed. The one little problem is that you're running out of sperm and I'm running out of quality eggs.

MARTIN: It'd be like you've been unfaithful.

CLAUDIA: Martin!

MARTIN: Metaphorically.

CLAUDIA: If all I ever am is metaphorically unfaithful, you're doing okay.

MARTIN: I'd rather adopt.

CLAUDIA: So the child isn't yours *or* mine?

MARTIN: In some weird way, that's fairer.

CLAUDIA: You bloody well know adoption's almost impossible.

MARTIN: I just don't want to be bringing up another guy's child.

CLAUDIA: You don't want me to have any child!

MARTIN: That's not true. Absolutely not true. I *wanted* this kid. As soon as I knew you were pregnant it really hit me. I wanted it as much as you.

CLAUDIA: Yeah, I know. Sorry.

MARTIN: What have you got against IVF?

CLAUDIA: It's intrusive and messy and it's got a hopeless success rate.

MARTIN: It's getting better all the time.

CLAUDIA: The other way's just so simple. A load of healthy sperm and zap.

MARTIN: As long as I've got *some* healthy sperm, IVF can work.

    CLAUDIA *wipes away the tears and looks at* MARTIN. *Then nods.*

CLAUDIA: Yeah, sorry. I want it be your child. Come here.

    MARTIN *sits beside her and she embraces him.*

Let's do IVF.

MARTIN: I want a kid too now. I really do. Once it started growing in there, suddenly… it all made sense.

    They kiss.

SCENE FOUR

The hospital waiting room. Two years later.

MARTIN *waits, looking nervous and worried.* CLAUDIA *enters. She's already in her operating theatre gown.* MARTIN *approaches her looking worried.*

CLAUDIA: What's wrong?

MARTIN: That room they put me in. Those magazines and videos. I can't do it anymore.

CLAUDIA: What?

MARTIN: The nurses are all out there listening.

CLAUDIA: Martin, I can assure that in this place the nurses are far too busy to be getting off on the sound of you wanking.

MARTIN: I can't do it.

CLAUDIA: Martin, they're just about to shove a very sharp object through the walls of my vagina to get to my few remaining eggs. It's an extremely painful and undignified process, so for God's sake, get back in that room and do your bloody bit.

MARTIN: Come back with me. I need some help.

CLAUDIA: Martin, I'm not feeling particularly romantic. Use the videos!

MARTIN: I hope you feel easy with the fact that the sperm starting your child is courtesy of some slutty porn star with one in her mouth and another up her rear.

CLAUDIA: Martin, stop whining. You've got the easy part. Go and do it!

MARTIN *mutters and turns away.*

And you've only got half an hour!

◆ ◆ ◆ ◆ ◆

SCENE FIVE

City café. Two weeks later.

MARGARET *waits for* CLAUDIA *at their usual café.* CLAUDIA *enters, looking excited. She kisses her mother warmly.*

MARGARET: No sign?

CLAUDIA: Fourteen days, no sign. I feel unbelievably fertile. I just know it's happened this time.

MARGARET: When's the test?

CLAUDIA: A few days more. Look, I know I've been optimistic before, but I know this time it's different. Somehow my body's telling me this is it.

MARGARET: I hope you're right.

CLAUDIA: Don't look so gloomy. It's happened. And thank God. I can't take much more of this. It's torture.

MARGARET: It sounds appalling.

CLAUDIA: It's a nightmare. Your whole life is taken over. You're shuttled between hospital and home, injected full of hormones, prodded, poked, invaded, monitored and treated as if you're a lobotomised incubator. You stare up at all the white coats and feel like yelling: 'Speak to me. I'm still more or less human.'

MARGARET: Awful.

CLAUDIA: You have no sense of who you are anymore. You've got nothing to add to any conversation. No opinions worth uttering. All you're obsessed with is your own fertility. The process has taken total control of you and you're at the mercy of white coats and fate.

MARGARET *says nothing.*

I'm barely hanging in there at work. They know I'm not pulling my weight, I hate it.

MARGARET: Do you really think you should go on?

CLAUDIA: I don't need to go on. This time it's worked.

MARGARET *is silent.*

I've said that before, haven't I? Probably deluding myself yet again. That's the cruellest part. The hormones make you feel as if you're bursting with fertility. Engorged. Your whole body's screaming 'pregnant, pregnant', and in your mind you're holding your baby's hand, mentally blissed-out as she takes her first wobbly steps. Then you bleed. Total devastation. Total. A whole future leeching out of you. And nobody understands. All that regimentation and humiliation all for nothing. [*She looks around and sighs.*] For a week or so after I can't even step outside. I'm scared some idiot will thrust a baby into my hands to make me feel 'better', and that I'll grab its legs and dash its brains out. You know there are much worse things happening to other people out there and you hate yourself for the self pity. But there's nothing you can do. The obsession washes everything else out of your mind.

MARGARET: Don't do another cycle. Nine's enough.

CLAUDIA: I was getting dressed in a cubicle a few weeks back after yet another vaginal ultrasound, and a woman went into the next cubicle and started howling. Not just crying. Howling. Huge sobs. Felt like they must be shaking her apart. I wanted to reach through the curtain and hold her hand, but I knew it wouldn't do any good. I sat there till she finished. Utter silence. It was worse than the sobs.

MARGARET: Don't do another cycle.

CLAUDIA: [*determined*] I won't need to do another cycle. This time it's really happened.

SCENE SIX

Claudia's place. Next night.

CLAUDIA *is sitting tensely, trying to read.*

MARTIN: Let's go out and eat.

CLAUDIA: I'll make something in a minute.

MARTIN: I'll do an omelette, or get some takeaway.

CLAUDIA: You're hungry, okay? I've got the message. Just wait a minute.

> MARTIN *simmers, controlling himself. She looks at him.*

Can you understand maybe why I'm a little tense?

MARTIN: [*suddenly angry*] You're always fucking tense!

CLAUDIA: I'm two days over. It might've happened.

> MARTIN *suddenly thumps the couch violently.*

MARTIN: You know what? I don't care anymore. By the time this bloody kid arrives, if it ever arrives, there'll be nothing left of our relationship in any case.

CLAUDIA: We've both been through a hell of a lot, but—

MARTIN: Nothing's worth going through the kind of life we're leading now.

> MARTIN *starts to leave.*

CLAUDIA: If you had any feelings at all you wouldn't deliberately try and upset me. Especially not right now.

> *He's gone.* CLAUDIA *remains on the couch staring sightlessly ahead.*

SCENE SEVEN

Claudia's place. Two days later.

CLAUDIA *is now sitting on the couch staring ahead.* MARTIN *sits at the other end. He turns to her.*

MARTIN: No!
CLAUDIA: Once more. I've got to try it once more.
MARTIN: No!
CLAUDIA: If I give up now, I'll hate myself the rest of my life.
MARTIN: You go anywhere near that fucking clinic and I'm out of here.
CLAUDIA: Martin—
MARTIN: Can you try and look at this rationally?
CLAUDIA: This is not about being rational! I'm not in control of this thing, it's in control of me.
MARTIN: It's fucking obsession and it's taken over your life!
CLAUDIA: Everywhere I look the world is full of babies and I want mine.
MARTIN: It's like an alien's taken over your body. And when you're not saying or doing something weird, you sit there, totally depressed.
CLAUDIA: I want mine!
MARTIN: Claudia, you're three parts crazy. Your partners are trying to think of a way to get you out of the firm. Can't you see that? You're three parts crazy!

   There's a silence.

SCENE EIGHT

City café. 2000. Some months later.

HELEN *waits for her sister.* CLAUDIA *appears. They kiss perfunctorily.*

HELEN: How are you?
CLAUDIA: Slowly getting my life back together.

ACT TWO

HELEN: Sorry we haven't seen much of each other.

There's a pause.

CLAUDIA: I'm never going to have a child.

HELEN: There's still time.

CLAUDIA: I'm forty-two. Nearly forty-three. And the chances are down to one in fifty per cycle. Martin had to finally point out that what I was doing was insane.

HELEN: A friend of a friend of mine was forty-four, and—

CLAUDIA: Helen, I don't want to hear any more of those stories.

There's a silence.

HELEN: How's Martin?

CLAUDIA: Obviously Mother told you his magazine went bust.

HELEN: Why 'obviously'?

CLAUDIA: You wouldn't have asked about him otherwise.

HELEN: You think I'm that vindictive?

There's a silence.

The truth is we're worried about you. Mother said it left you with a mountain of debt.

CLAUDIA: His magazine was the last radical voice left in this country.

HELEN: There are positives.

CLAUDIA looks at her, frowning.

Not having a child. They do limit your freedom. In all kinds of ways. And there's not a day passes that you don't go through agonies about their happiness and safety. And the first few years are totally hellish.

CLAUDIA looks at her steadily.

CLAUDIA: Can we talk about Kelly?

HELEN: Odd timing.

CLAUDIA's look asks for clarification.

You can't have your own child so you want to talk about Kelly?

CLAUDIA: I just think it's ridiculous and appalling that you've tried to put a black ban on us communicating.

HELEN: Which you've both apparently ignored.

CLAUDIA: Helen, I'm not trying to 'steal' her from you.

HELEN: It's all about you. Always about you. Can't you begin to appreciate how vulnerable I feel?

CLAUDIA: You're her mother. You'll always be her mother. But sooner or later she's got to know the truth.

HELEN: The minute she knows it she'll choose you.

CLAUDIA: Helen!

HELEN: That's why you want her to know.

CLAUDIA: She'll simply realise she has two people who care deeply about her and she'll be all the better for it. I can't believe that you feel this threatened.

HELEN: Well, just think about it for once. You're the genuine article. I'm the fake.

CLAUDIA: This doesn't have to be a competition. Let her know the truth and I guarantee she'll think all the more of you.

Doris Younane (left) as Helen and Maria Theodorakis as Claudia in the 2003 Melbourne Theatre Company production. (Photo: Jeff Busby)

HELEN: I don't want her to know. Not yet.

CLAUDIA: You're not the only stakeholder here.

HELEN: In your mind you've never really handed her over, have you?

CLAUDIA: No, not totally. And it was crazy of both of us to ever think I could.

HELEN: And you're trying to tell me this isn't a competition?

CLAUDIA: At some level it *has* to be. You can't totally deny what your heart's telling you.

HELEN: I always knew this was the price I was going to have to pay.

CLAUDIA: She's my child and I want her to know that! It doesn't mean I want to take her away. It doesn't mean you won't always be her mother. I just want her to know!

The two sisters glare at each other. HELEN *gets up and walks off.*

SCENE NINE

City café. Some days later.

MARGARET *waits for* HELEN. HELEN *comes in looking flustered.*

MARGARET: What's wrong?

HELEN: You name it. Claudia's threatening to tell Kelly I'm not her mother and Mark's telling me I can't go back to university.

MARGARET: Why?

HELEN: He said: 'You're nearly forty-seven. Don't be such an idiot.'

MARGARET: To hell with him. There are women in their seventies doing brilliantly.

HELEN: If I keep on about it, he'll just start yelling.

MARGARET: Yell back.

HELEN: He's just scared he'll lose his housekeeper, cook and entertainer.

MARGARET: He's had that all for free for long enough. I'm absolutely delighted. What made you decide?

HELEN: I started reading Kelly's school history essays, then her textbooks, then I got totally hooked. And I thought I've spent so many years playing support to Mark and Kelly and everyone else. It's my turn for a life.

MARGARET: Bravo.

HELEN: And I obviously won't have a daughter for much longer, so why not?

MARGARET: If you really believe that, mightn't it be better to face your fears and tell her?

HELEN: Claudia's an incredibly successful high-flying lawyer. Why would Kelly ever choose me?

MARGARET: Because you've been a loving, concerned and very hard working mother. Every time I look at you in action I feel guilty all over again.

HELEN: Mum, I'm sorry I've given you such a hard time.

MARGARET: [*shrugging*] You had cause.

HELEN: She treats me like dirt.

Doris Younane (left) as Helen and Deidre Rubenstein as Margaret in the 2003 Melbourne Theatre Company production. (Photo: Jeff Busby)

MARGARET: However rebellious she is on the surface, that young girl of yours knows which side her bread is buttered on.
HELEN: Claudia is so 'progressive'.
MARGARET: Or dogmatic.
HELEN: I *have* been so… conservative, politically. Echoing every opinion Mark ever has.
MARGARET: Well, don't do it anymore.
HELEN: I don't. But I'll never be as 'trendy' as that bloody queen of political correctness Claudia.
MARGARET: Kelly knows who her mother is, believe me.

HELEN *is moved by her mother's support. She leans across and puts her head on* MARGARET*'s shoulder.* MARGARET *strokes her hair.*

HELEN: Don't let Claudia tell her. Please.
MARGARET: She's not about to.
HELEN: I couldn't take it right now.

SCENE TEN

Claudia's apartment. That evening.

CLAUDIA *is reading the paper.* MARTIN *comes in looking frazzled.*

CLAUDIA: Any luck?
MARTIN: No. Who wants a burnt-out cartoonist?
CLAUDIA: You're qualified.
MARTIN: I haven't taught for… nearly fifteen years.
CLAUDIA: Did you try in the secondary system?
MARTIN: The secondary system? Spend the rest of my days trying to control twelve-year-old psychopaths?
CLAUDIA: All right. Go get a job shifting furniture, or a courier, or a taxi driver.
MARTIN: I'm an artist. I fucking paint!
CLAUDIA: I thought even you realised that little dream was over.
MARTIN: You never believed that I had any talent, did you?

CLAUDIA: Yes I did. Then.
MARTIN: Great. No talent, so go and teach twelve-year-olds.
CLAUDIA: I don't care what you do, Martin. Work it out yourself.
MARTIN: We can't all charge five hundred dollars an hour.
CLAUDIA: No, you have to be worth it.
MARTIN: The world's really easy from where you stand.
CLAUDIA: No, it isn't. And you don't make it any easier.
MARTIN: So I can't earn, I'm no use, so get out. Is that the message?
CLAUDIA: I've listened to you, your raving, your paranoia and your excuses for eighteen years. Nothing you've tried has worked and you know something? It's not society's fault, it's not my fault, guess what—it's yours.
MARTIN: You're never going to forgive me, are you?
CLAUDIA: For what?
MARTIN: Sperm count pathetic. Not a real man.
CLAUDIA: You had more than enough sperm for IVF. The eggs fertilised. Every bloody time. They just wouldn't implant. *I* was the problem.
MARTIN: You can't obsess about it all your life. It's time to move on!
CLAUDIA: I want to move on.

> *She turns away from him. The meaning of her body language dawns on him.*

MARTIN: Without me?

> *She says nothing.*

[*Angrily*] Just like that? After all these years?

> *She still doesn't respond.*

This is crazy! I've given everything to this relationship for nearly twenty years! And just when I'm at my lowest point you dump me. Without a word of warning. Don't I mean *anything* to you? Don't our years together mean *something*?
CLAUDIA: Martin—
MARTIN: What am I? Nothing to you? Nothing? Just a bit of dogshit you scrape off your boots!
CLAUDIA: It's interesting, Martin.
MARTIN: What's interesting?

CLAUDIA: The one thing you haven't said is: 'I can't bear to split up because I still love you'.
MARTIN: I do. Of course I do.
CLAUDIA: [*shaking her head*] It's all about your wounded pride.

SCENE ELEVEN

Claudia's place. Evening. A few months later. 2001.

KELLY, *an attractive and vivacious young eighteen-year-old sits on a sofa smoking a joint. She's obviously done it before as she gets the maximum kick out of the available cannabis. The music on the hi-fi system is the latest rave-type music. She gets up and dances wildly to the beat. The door opens and* CLAUDIA *comes in and stares at her niece.* KELLY *looks at her aunt and grins as* CLAUDIA *sniffs the air.* KELLY *dances across and turns the music off.*

KELLY: Hi Claudie.

She gives CLAUDIA *an affectionate kiss and hands her the joint.*

CLAUDIA: Hi.

CLAUDIA *looks at the joint, then hands it back.*

KELLY: Don't be cross.

CLAUDIA *moves across and picks up a male coat that's draped across a sofa.*

CLAUDIA: Whose is this?
KELLY: Simon's.
CLAUDIA: What happened to Russell?
KELLY: Russell's a bore.
CLAUDIA: So, is Simon still here?
KELLY: [*indicating the coat*] No, he just sort've floated away.
CLAUDIA: [*sniffing the air*] I'm sure he did.

CLAUDIA *picks up one of two empty glasses and sniffs it.*

KELLY: We had a little bit of your whisky.
CLAUDIA: So I see.
KELLY: We didn't use your bed.
CLAUDIA: Thanks.
KELLY: I'm sorry.

But she isn't as her laughter illustrates.

CLAUDIA: What are you laughing at?
KELLY: You look so shocked. [*She waves the remainder of the joint she's smoking.*] Don't try and tell me you haven't had one of these before.
CLAUDIA: When I gave you the key to this place it was so you could come here and study.
KELLY: Claudie, don't be cross. I had a fabulous afternoon. Amazing.
CLAUDIA: What about your lecture?
KELLY: I had it here.
CLAUDIA: Here?
KELLY: [*nodding*] Simon's my lecturer.

CLAUDIA *sits down on a sofa.*

CLAUDIA: You're sleeping with your lecturer?
KELLY: [*laughing*] We didn't sleep, I assure you.
CLAUDIA: You know that's a dangerous sort of area.
KELLY: Not these days, Claudie. I don't think anyone gives a damn.
CLAUDIA: Really?
KELLY: Moral standards are arbitrary social constructions.
CLAUDIA: And if he gives your essays preferential treatment?
KELLY: Claudie, it happens all the time. Fee-paying students are passed when they shouldn't be because the universities need the money.
CLAUDIA: It wouldn't worry you if the reason you passed was because you slept with your lecturer?
KELLY: No.
CLAUDIA: Call me old-fashioned but I happen to believe that those with power shouldn't abuse it.
KELLY: Well, they do. All the time. In every way they can. Then use all kinds of dodgy rhetoric to justify it.
CLAUDIA: Which doesn't make it right.
KELLY: What's right?

ACT TWO

CLAUDIA: [*getting angry*] There are rules of decent behaviour, whether you want to acknowledge them or not.

KELLY: Claudie, I love that you want to believe in a world of moral absolutes, but my generation knows that's a fantasy world.

CLAUDIA: If the world's totally without moral standards then God help us.

KELLY: It's all a game.

CLAUDIA: Sleeping with your lecturers? That's part of the game?

KELLY: Simon has power over me. I use my wits to lessen that power.

CLAUDIA: It seems like you're using a bit more than your wits.

KELLY: Claudie. It's all a game. Even history is a story we invent about the past to suit our needs in the present.

CLAUDIA: No! History is something that actually happened.

KELLY: You're sounding more and more like my mother. She's being taught by one of the last of the 'objective' history dinosaurs and she says *exactly* the same sort of things as you.

CLAUDIA: I'm glad.

KELLY: What a nightmare. Everywhere I go on campus, there's Mum.

CLAUDIA: Don't be so horrible.

KELLY: She looks as if she's off to a charity ball. Hair like a volcanic eruption.

CLAUDIA: Kelly!

KELLY: The corporate wife reporting for brain restoral.

CLAUDIA: Thank God she is.

KELLY: Thankfully hardly anyone on campus knows I'm related to her.

CLAUDIA: Kelly.

KELLY: She's got her own group. The menopausal mums.

CLAUDIA: [*trying to stop grinning*] Stop it.

KELLY: They hop around like a flock of lorikeets squawking at each other.

CLAUDIA: It took a lot of courage for her to stand up to your father and go back.

KELLY: It's just *such* an embarrassment.

    KELLY *pours herself another whisky.*

CLAUDIA: Kelly, I'm really uneasy about you using my place for this sort of thing.

KELLY: What sort of thing?

CLAUDIA: Smoking pot, drinking, reducing power differentials.

KELLY: You're starting to sound like Mum.

CLAUDIA: We're both concerned.

KELLY: You always understood that I needed more room than she'd ever let me have.

CLAUDIA: You're pushing it too far.

KELLY: Claudie, I'm not a fool.

CLAUDIA: If you want to see Simon, do it at his place.

KELLY: Can't.

> CLAUDIA *looks at* KELLY *who looks away.*

CLAUDIA: He's married?

KELLY: In a relationship.

CLAUDIA: Kelly!

KELLY: I'll handle it.

CLAUDIA: I don't like this.

KELLY: It's fine. I'll handle it.

> CLAUDIA *looks at her, worried and dubious.*

CLAUDIA: The world isn't just about power, Kelly. It's a lot about power, I'll give you that, but it's not *all* it's about.

KELLY: What is it about?

CLAUDIA: Needing other people. Trusting them. Sometimes it's even about love.

KELLY: Love?

CLAUDIA: It does exist.

KELLY: Have you ever *really* loved anyone?

> CLAUDIA *looks at her and nods.*

CLAUDIA: Yes.

> CLAUDIA *can't articulate that it's* KELLY *she loves, but* KELLY *is unsettled by the intensity of the reply.*

KELLY: Hey, don't worry. I'm going to be fine.

> CLAUDIA *stands looking at her and nods. Hoping she's right.*

◆ ◆ ◆ ◆ ◆

SCENE TWELVE

A hospice. October 2001

MARGARET *is in bed looking pale.* HELEN *is sitting by her side.*

HELEN: Would you like some more water?
MARGARET: No, I'm fine. How's Kelly?
HELEN: How would I know?
MARGARET: You go to the same university.
HELEN: She snubs me. I'm an embarrassment.
MARGARET: I'm sure she doesn't.
HELEN: Sees me coming and turns away.
MARGARET: She's still living at home?
HELEN: Nominally. She spends every second night at Claudia's.
MARGARET: It's much closer to university.
HELEN: She prefers it there.

> MARGARET *sighs*.

Sorry to burden you with this.
MARGARET: Let it out.
HELEN: It's just so crushing. I've done all the hard work bringing her up and it counts for nothing. She really might as well be Claudia's child.
MARGARET: I've told you. Kelly knows who her mother is.
HELEN: [*angrily*] She damn well should. I did the sleepless nights, the fevers, the croup, and the non-stop shuttle to every damn life-enrichment activity on offer. I was the one who sat on her bed at night during the floods of tears about the schoolyard snubs, the teachers who picked on her, and her father's occasional hopeless attempts at discipline. I'm the one who did the thousands upon thousands of hours of unpaid thankless drudgery called 'raising' the child. If she's going to dump me after all of that then good bloody riddance.
MARGARET: Exactly. Good for you.
HELEN: I love her, but I'm not going to cringe and bend to her every whim out of fear I'll lose her, because if I do, I will.

MARGARET: Exactly. That little tyke gets away with murder by playing you two off against each other. If I had the strength I'd box her bloody ears.

HELEN: She was totally spoilt. Too late to undo the damage now, but she's not getting away with any more of it.

MARGARET: Good for you. And don't weaken. Stick to your guns.

HELEN: Don't worry. I will. No more Mrs Nice Mum. Finish.

MARGARET: Great!

> MARGARET *clutches* HELEN's *hand and gives it an encouraging squeeze.* CLAUDIA *comes in.*

CLAUDIA: Hi Mum. Hi Helen. [*To* MARGARET] How are you feeling?

MARGARET: Weak.

CLAUDIA: Pain?

MARGARET: [*shaking her head*] They keep me on this morphine drip.

CLAUDIA: [*to* HELEN] Kelly tells me you're doing very well at uni.

HELEN: I'm surprised she even knows.

CLAUDIA: I'm sure she's proud.

HELEN: She won't even come near me on campus.

CLAUDIA: She's a typical teenager. Wrapped up in her own little world.

HELEN: Well, you'd know, wouldn't you? We never see her.

CLAUDIA: Helen, don't start this.

HELEN: Has her latest boyfriend turned up at your place?

CLAUDIA: No.

HELEN: You're lucky. No wonder she doesn't want me on the same campus.

CLAUDIA: Why?

HELEN: I saw him come to pick her up. Hideous creature.

CLAUDIA: Really?

HELEN: Bouncer at a nightclub. Steroid-pumped muscles and Raybans. Drives a BMW with tinted windows.

CLAUDIA: Bouncer?

HELEN: And three guesses how he made that sort of money. Drugs. He pushes to teenage kids at the nightclub.

CLAUDIA: I thought she was going out with someone on campus.

HELEN: No, she's going out with a foul-mouthed drug runner twice her age. And if you can possibly find the time, Mark and I would like you to come round and discuss this, and a few other things.

CLAUDIA: Fine. Next week?

HELEN: Tonight. I'll try and come in on Thursday, Mum.

MARGARET: That'd be nice.

HELEN: Sorry I can't stay longer, but I've got a tutorial.

HELEN kisses her mother and leaves with a curt nod to CLAUDIA. There's a silence as CLAUDIA looks at her mother.

MARGARET: I wish you two would get this Kelly thing worked out.

CLAUDIA: If Helen wasn't so insanely possessive it'd be fine.

MARGARET: Helen said she's staying at your place every second night.

CLAUDIA: [*shaking her head*] I'm just the alibi. She's with... whoever.

MARGARET: The bouncer chap?

CLAUDIA: I didn't know anything about him. She told me she'd finally found someone who was different and exciting and she was in love and had to be with him.

MARGARET: I don't think you should cover for her anymore.

CLAUDIA: Now I know what's going on, I won't.

MARGARET: Be firm with her. She can twist you round her little finger.

CLAUDIA: Has she been to visit you yet?

MARGARET: Why would she? I'm not different or exciting.

CLAUDIA: The little rat.

There's a pause.

So how are you really?

MARGARET: Sad. I wish I'd done a lot of things differently. Been a better mother to you two.

CLAUDIA: You started slowly, but you've gained momentum.

MARGARET: Really?

CLAUDIA: Without you acting as a one-person permanent peace mission, Helen and I would have strangled each other by now.

MARGARET: I *was* terrible in the early years.

CLAUDIA: [*laughing*] You *were* pretty average. And some of those 'menfriends' of yours we had to put up with were very, very average.

MARGARET: Oh God, weren't they.

CLAUDIA: I know exactly where Kelly gets her taste in men from.

MARGARET: I had this thing that prisoners were victims of capitalism.

[*She shakes her head at her naivety.*] And most of them were duds. Your father did have one talent I missed.

CLAUDIA: Are you—worried?

MARGARET: About dying? [*She shakes her head.*] As Gough Whitlam said: 'It's time'. But I am terrified about the pain. If it gets worse. I was never good with pain. Talk to Helen and Mark about it. Please.

CLAUDIA nods.

CLAUDIA: Can I do anything for you?

MARGARET: Hold my hand.

CLAUDIA takes her hand and they sit there in silence.

SCENE THIRTEEN

Helen and Mark's place. That night.

HELEN *places a tray of canapes on a table.* MARK *brings two bottles of wine into the room.* HELEN *already has a vodka and tonic in her hand.*

MARK: What's she drink, red or white?

HELEN: I don't know.

MARK: Martinis. Doesn't she have martinis?

HELEN: Try and be polite.

MARK: I'm not going to put up with her left-wing shit if she launches into that stuff yet again.

HELEN: Just be calm.

The doorbell rings. MARK *looks at* HELEN, *who goes to the door.* MARK *scowls and pours himself a whisky.* HELEN *enters with* CLAUDIA.

MARK: Hi Claudia.

CLAUDIA: Hi Mark.

MARK: Martini?

CLAUDIA: Just water thanks.

MARK: Ice.

CLAUDIA: No thanks.

HELEN thrusts the canapes at her. CLAUDIA *shakes her head.*

HELEN: Sorry to drag you out, but Mum's been rabbiting on about finishing it before the pain gets too bad. She wants us to talk to the doctors.

MARK: Which I'm quite happy to do if you want me to.

CLAUDIA: I've done it. They say she needn't be scared. The pain management is excellent and they'll just keep increasing her dose as required until the end.

HELEN: She really won't ever be in bad pain?

CLAUDIA: No.

HELEN: They're not just saying that?

CLAUDIA: No.

HELEN: What a relief. I keep saying what a bad mother she is, but oh God, I love her.

CLAUDIA: So do I.

The sisters embrace.

HELEN: How will we cope when she's gone?

CLAUDIA: She's very worried we both get the paintings and furniture we like. I tried to tell her not to worry, and we'll sort it out, but you know what she's like.

HELEN: You take what you want. Your taste is more hers than mine.

MARK: While you're here, Helen and I are very concerned about this bouncer guy Kelly's seeing. Has she bought him to your place?

CLAUDIA: No.

MARK: He's a drug dealer. He's been in prison.

CLAUDIA: For what?

HELEN: Assault, grievous bodily harm, drugs. She told us. Proudly.

MARK: But he's not bad, of course. He just had a rough upbringing. He's just a victim of society. All that rubbish you taught her.

HELEN: Mark, don't let's start on this.

MARK: Do you think she'd be attracted to gutter life if you had've left *us* to bring her up?

HELEN: Mark.

MARK: And when she's not consorting with criminals she's abusing us because we don't happen to believe that every boatload of refugees headed for our shores should be welcomed with open arms.

HELEN: Mark.

MARK: Terrorists, criminals, who cares. Welcome them all.

HELEN: Mark, not tonight.

MARK: You don't think we have a right to protect our own borders?

CLAUDIA: Mark, the refugees that are coming here are desperate people fleeing from some of the worst regimes on earth.

MARK: That's the left's story.

CLAUDIA: [*angrily*] No, Mark. It's the real story. It's what the investigators who assess them eventually admit.

MARK: Have you bothered to listen to the radio lately? Read the newspapers?

HELEN: Mark, calm down.

MARK: No, I won't.

CLAUDIA: Yes, I've been reading the newspapers and I've been ashamed to the point of despair.

MARK: You've read about the pack rapes by Muslims of Christian girls. And how they taunt them for being Christians as they're doing it. At knife point. And you want more of these people here?

CLAUDIA: I've been reading another story. About the mother whose three young daughters drowned when their boat sank.

MARK: It's not Australia's fault. It's the fault of those bloody people smugglers who take money and jam them into unseaworthy boats.

CLAUDIA: The reason she was on that boat, Mark?

MARK: It was her choice.

CLAUDIA: Not really. Her husband's already here. His boat made it and he was assessed as a genuine refugee. But then our deeply humanitarian government changed the law so that families of even genuine refugees could never join them. Never.

MARK: You've got to draw a line.

CLAUDIA: The mother tried to hang on to her daughters as long as she could but after twenty-three hours in the water she was barely alive herself. And instead of allowing her to join her husband here she's refused entry. And he's told that if he goes to Indonesia to join her he'll never be allowed back in.

HELEN: It was horrible. I felt genuinely ashamed to be Australian.

CLAUDIA: It was inhumanity on a level that this country has never *ever* descended to before.

MARK: You make one exception to the rules and smart lawyers'll have us flooded with them.

CLAUDIA: What are you so terrified of, Mark? Do you really think the only rapists in Australia are Muslims? Do you really think that a few thousand desperate people a year are going to make us terrified to go out at night? What are we? The most panic-prone nation on earth?

HELEN: That footage of that woman. Distraught out of her brain. It was horrible.

CLAUDIA: She only wanted one thing. To be reunited with the father of her three drowned girls. And what did we say? No. Are you made of bloody stone, Mark? Can you imagine how you might feel if anything ever happened to Kelly and you two weren't allowed to be with each other?

HELEN: Don't say that, Claudia.

CLAUDIA: Think about it, Mark. And try and get some idea into your stupid skull just how appallingly callous you're being.

She slams down her glass, turns and goes. The door slams after her. There's silence.

MARK: I still say we've got to draw a line.

HELEN: Mark, just shut up!

SCENE FOURTEEN

Claudia's place. Next afternoon.

KELLY *is again dancing to her music. She has a joint in one hand and a glass of whisky in the other.* CLAUDIA *comes in and surveys the scene, then goes across and turns the music off.* KELLY *swings around.*

KELLY: Hi.

CLAUDIA: Kelly, I think you'd better give me my key back.

KELLY: Claudie, don't be shitty at me.

CLAUDIA: You didn't tell me about this new boyfriend of yours.

KELLY: Claudie, don't say 'boyfriend'. It's so… eighties.

CLAUDIA: Whatever. You didn't tell me about him.

KELLY: He's fine.

CLAUDIA: Your mother says he's a drug dealer.

KELLY: He sells a bit of ecstasy, for God's sake. It shouldn't even be illegal.

CLAUDIA: And he's violent.

KELLY: He stands up for himself. He's no middle-class wimp.

CLAUDIA: I'm covering for you, Kelly. I'm telling your mother you're here at nights staying with me. I want my key back.

KELLY: Take your fucking key back! You're just like Mum.

She fishes in her bag and hurls the key on the table.

CLAUDIA: And you might visit your grandmother once before she dies!

KELLY: I'm going to. I've been flat out.

CLAUDIA: [*indicating the empty glass and the joint*] So I see.

KELLY: I just can't hack seeing someone dying.

CLAUDIA: The visit's for her sake, not yours.

KELLY: I can't steel myself to go to that fucking death house.

CLAUDIA: The truth is you can't be bothered.

KELLY: Okay, okay. I'll go.

CLAUDIA: Soon.

KELLY: Who do you think you are, ordering me around? You're not my mother!

CLAUDIA: [*suddenly bursting out*] Actually, honey, I am.

KELLY: What?

CLAUDIA: I am.

KELLY: What the fuck are you talking about?

CLAUDIA: Your mother had no eggs. I was inseminated with your father's sperm. I conceived you, carried you, and bore you. I thought I was doing your mother a favour, but boy was I wrong.

KELLY: Is this some kind of sick joke?

CLAUDIA: It's turning out that way, because all we've produced between the two of us is a self-obsessed, amoral, pain in the arse.

> KELLY *stares at her.*

KELLY: This is heavy.

CLAUDIA: What's it matter? History is just a story we invent for ourselves about the past. Tell yourself you're an orphan and you're free of both of us.

KELLY: You're my mother?

CLAUDIA: Not in the sense that finally matters.

KELLY: Of course it *matters*! Why wasn't I told?!

CLAUDIA: Because your mother thought you might stop loving her. I'm not sure she cares anymore.

> KELLY *stares at her, then turns angrily and goes.*

SCENE FIFTEEN

Margaret's room in hospital. Soon after.

MARGARET *looks up as* KELLY *walks in.*

MARGARET: Well hello, stranger.

KELLY: Sorry. I meant to come earlier. It's just that this sort of thing… really upsets me.

MARGARET: Dying?

KELLY: Don't say it. Please.

MARGARET: It's part of the deal.

KELLY: Are you…?

MARGARET: In pain? No. Not at all.

> KELLY *starts to cry.*

Hey. I'm feeling fine.

KELLY: Did you know?

> MARGARET *looks at her.*

That Claudia is my mother?

MARGARET: Biological mother. Yes.

KELLY: The horrible thing is that I've always secretly liked her better.

MARGARET: Girls always like their aunts better. You know why? Because their aunts never have to say 'no'.

KELLY: What am I supposed to do now?

MARGARET: Think yourself lucky. Parents are the only ones in the world who'll ever offer unconditional love. And you've got three.

KELLY: I know I should love Helen more but she's so *conservative*.

MARGARET: Because she's worried that you're going out with a drug dealer?

KELLY: God, they're both onto me about that.

MARGARET: Good.

KELLY: I'm finishing with him tonight.

MARGARET: Promise.

KELLY: Absolutely. I know he's bad news, I just wasn't going to admit it to them.

    MARGARET *smiles.*

Deidre Rubenstein (left) as Margaret and Asher Keddie as Kelly in the 2003 Melbourne Theatre Company production. (Photo: Jeff Busby)

ACT TWO 73

I've been a bit of a pain lately, haven't I?
MARGARET: Oh, only about eighteen years.
KELLY: I don't even believe half of what I'm saying and I still say it. Why is that?
MARGARET: [*smiling*] Shock value. You love to be noticed.
KELLY: [*nodding*] I guess.
MARGARET: [*nodding*] I was just the same. My mother used to shake her head at me in despair and say: 'You know what you are? A bloody little show-off.'
KELLY: I really do love... Helen. I just can't show it.
MARGARET: Call her Mum. She's earned it.
KELLY: I just can't show it.
MARGARET: Try a bit harder. She's going to need it. Especially now.
KELLY: [*nodding*] Gran, I don't want you to die.
MARGARET: I would have liked to have lasted a little longer. Long enough to see how you turn out.
KELLY: Are you worried?
MARGARET: Not particularly. We show-offs usually do okay in the end.
KELLY: I'll do okay. Believe me.
MARGARET: Start by getting rid of Mr Rayban.
KELLY: I am. Tonight.

MARGARET *holds out her hand for* KELLY. KELLY *takes it.*

SCENE SIXTEEN

Hospital corridor. Early that morning.

HELEN *and* MARK *sit in the waiting area. Not looking at each other. Strain on their faces.* CLAUDIA *approaches. They look up at her.*

MARK: If she dies, you deserve to rot in hell.
CLAUDIA: What have they said?
HELEN: [*distraught*] Nothing. That's the bloody problem. Nothing.
CLAUDIA: Do they know what it is? What drugs she's taken?

MARK: Ecstasy, alcohol and dehydration. That's all it needs.
HELEN: She collapsed at a rave party.
MARK: The bouncer brought her here, then fled.
CLAUDIA: They've given you *no* indication of how she is?
MARK: They just say they're doing everything possible.
CLAUDIA: [*distraught*] Oh God. Don't let her die. Don't let her die.

>   HELEN *and* CLAUDIA *suddenly embrace in a desperate attempt to find solace.* MARK *looks away.*

SCENE SEVENTEEN

A rocky outcrop overlooking Sydney Harbour. Some months later.

MARTIN *sits by himself watching something happen below him.* CLAUDIA *climbs up beside him and stands watching also.*

MARTIN: It is a wonderful place to have your ashes spread.
CLAUDIA: She loved the view.
MARTIN: I think if anyone could be bothered spreading my ashes, this is the place I'll nominate.
CLAUDIA: I'm sure your new lady'll do it for you.

>   MARTIN *makes a hand gesture indicating that that's not at all certain.* MARK *and* HELEN *climb up beside them and stand looking down.*

So what are you doing now?
MARTIN: Website design.
CLAUDIA: Lots of money?
MARTIN: [*shaking his head*] Field's too crowded. Luckily my new 'lady' is a doctor.

>   KELLY *appears, still looking down at the view below.*

KELLY: I hope those really *were* Gran's ashes.
HELEN: What do you mean?
KELLY: I read somewhere they just shovel any old ashes into the container.

HELEN: Kelly!

KELLY: Saves them money.

MARK: We paid that funeral lot a fortune. They better've been the right ones!

KELLY: It really wouldn't matter, would it?

HELEN: Don't say things like that!

KELLY: Sorry... Mum. I'm sure they were Gran's.

HELEN: Then why get me all worked up?

KELLY: [*grinning*] According to Gran, because I'm a bloody little show-off.

CLAUDIA: Thank God someone told you at last.

MARTIN: Is it true your mother's doing better than you are at uni, Kelly?

HELEN: Yes, and she can't stand it.

KELLY: Yeah, only because you take stone-age subjects and parrot back everything your lecturers say.

HELEN: At least I still try and find tangible evidence for every assertion I make.

KELLY: It's called deluding yourself.

HELEN: No, actually it's called scholarship.

KELLY: We've scattered Gran. We don't have to hang around all day.

HELEN: Kelly!

KELLY: Look, I loved her too, but she's not going to be timing us. I've got to get a present for Justine's nineteenth.

MARK: Just make sure I don't get too big a shock when it shows up on my credit card.

KELLY: Dad. I'm going to pay you back.

MARK: Yeah, sure.

KELLY: I'm getting a job. Cocktail waitress.

MARK: Yeah, sure.

KELLY: See you, Claudie. Good to see you again, Martin.

MARTIN: Likewise.

> KELLY *and* HELEN *go.* MARK *watches them, then turns to* CLAUDIA *and* MARTIN.

MARK: I was glad they finally let that woman into the country.

CLAUDIA *looks puzzled.*

To be with her husband. The refugee woman whose three children were drowned.

CLAUDIA: Oh, yes. Long overdue.

MARK: I still think we've got a right to protect our borders.

CLAUDIA: Right.

MARK: But I have to admit that if I was living in some third-world shithole with a family, I'd be trying my hardest to get out too. Good to see you again, Martin.

MARTIN: Likewise.

MARK *gives* CLAUDIA *an awkward kiss and goes. They watch him.*

CLAUDIA: Thanks for coming.

MARTIN: I liked your mother. Things okay?

CLAUDIA: Grieving a little.

MARTIN: She was quite a woman.

CLAUDIA: Not so much for her. She lived a life.

MARTIN *looks at her.*

For Kelly.

MARTIN: She's really fond of you. I can tell.

CLAUDIA: I guess there was a selfish little part of me hoping that when she found out the truth she'd be… even more fond of me.

MARTIN: No?

CLAUDIA: [*shrugging*] Hard to say. I think she's still sorting it out. I hear your new young wife is pregnant?

MARTIN: [*embarrassed*] I was going to tell you.

CLAUDIA: Even a low sperm count is no impediment if you catch them young enough, I guess. Plenty of good eggs left at thirty-two.

MARTIN: Try not to be so bitter.

CLAUDIA: It's pretty hard, Martin. I still have dreams that I've had our baby. I'm holding her and I've got tears of joy in my eyes, but then I look down and it's turning into something like living sand and dribbling through my fingers.

MARTIN: I'm sorry. I really am. [*He looks around prior to making his escape.*] Well.

CLAUDIA: All my friends were saying they were never having kids. Financial independence, career. That's what it was all about. Then suddenly I was thirty-seven and I looked around and every one of them had managed to slip a child or two in somehow. I felt totally betrayed. But finally it was my call, wasn't it?
MARTIN: I shouldn't have come.
CLAUDIA: I'm not always self-pitying. I do have a life. I am coping. Most of the time quite well. Very well. But you'll understand if I don't send you a card when the new arrival blesses your life.

He nods and goes. CLAUDIA *sighs, then looks down at the place where her mother's ashes were spread.* KELLY *comes back onstage.*

KELLY: Can I get a lift with you?
CLAUDIA: Weren't you going with your mother?
KELLY: I'm sick of her picking on me.
CLAUDIA: Sorry. You were rude to her.
KELLY: It was a joke. She's just so touchy. [*Beat.*] I still haven't sorted this thing out in my head.
CLAUDIA: Neither have any of us. Helen says your new man isn't much of an improvement on your last.
KELLY: Hey! I made a stupid mistake and I nearly died. I'm not about to let it happen again.
CLAUDIA: A rock musician?
KELLY: Rock? No one plays rock anymore.
CLAUDIA: Whatever, just don't do it to us again.
KELLY: Oh Migod! Gran says I was lucky to have two mums. I don't think so. Oh God, there's Mum Number One beckoning. Better go.
CLAUDIA: Weren't you coming with me?
KELLY: I should go with Mum. [*Realising what she's said*] Does it upset you when I call her that?
CLAUDIA: No. Of course not. She is. And I'm rather glad to be number two.

KELLY *hugs* CLAUDIA *and runs off.* CLAUDIA *watches her go.*

More than you could know.

THE END

SOULMATES

Jacki Weaver as Heather in the 2002 Sydney Theatre Company production. (Photo: Tracey Schramm)

Introduction

Kathy Lette

When my friend David Williamson wrote to say that he'd put me in a play and did I mind, my only thought was casting. Nicole Kidman sprang to mind. As did Cate Blanchett. But let's face it, were they *beautiful* enough? I did offer to play the part myself—a suggestion which was met with the same enthusiasm as a yeast infection. Obviously, any more glib comments and the only cast I'd be in would be made of plaster. My only stipulations for the character of best-selling novelist Katie Best, were that she give her readers quip-lash on a regular basis and have fabulous footwear. I also suggested she get to sleep with Brad Pitt or George Clooney a lot, when she wasn't too busy picking up her Nobel Prize for Literature, that is—but by that time, David, strangely, seemed to have changed his email address.

The play's theme was very close to my heart. (That thing we girls wear on our sleeves.) High art versus low. The Literary World is full of Conan the Grammarians; academics who've been at University so long they've got ivy growing up the backs of their legs and what they've graduated in is Advanced Smugness. Believe me, to be a literary critic you must be born with a Condescension Chromosome. These are people who suffer from *high* Self-Esteem. A literary critic's basic premise, especially a certain species from Melbourne, is that unless an author is hooked up intravenously to a thesaurus, then he or she is not worth reading. They refuse to accept that literature can be profound, but also pleasurable; an experience which lifts the spirits while engaging the mind. This is not a new phenomenon. *Cold Comfort Farm*, *Diary of a Nobody*, all of P. G. Wodehouse and E. M. Foster and Mrs Gaskell (whose novel *Cranford* is set almost in the same period and place as *Middlemarch*, but which was never taken as seriously as work by the more sombre George Eliot) —all writers who did not think optimism was some kind of eye disease, were never given the critical success they deserved. If only critics would heed Dr Johnson, who observed that 'the true end of literature is to enable the reader better to enjoy life or better to endure it'.

Of course, David Williamson has suffered this same kind of elitist disdain from theatre critics. His work has been routinely savaged for being too 'frivolous' or 'low-brow'. The public, however, have voted with their feet, flocking to see his plays for over three decades. In many ways, David Williamson has been the voice of Australia; chronicling our national faults and foibles with wry insights and a fierce intelligence. His plays have been a cultural thermometer, taking our psychological temperature and then making a theatrical diagnosis. And always with wit, warmth, wisdom and his trademark wise-cracking humour.

Scientists tell us that laughter is innate; it originates in the oldest part of the brain, the hypothalamus. Biologists maintain that laughter increases our biological fitness. Anthropologists have revealed that the Eskimos hold laughing competitions and women, in all cultures, laugh more often than men do, especially in all-female groups. If a cultural survey was undertaken, I feel sure we'd discover that Australians laugh more often than other nationalities. Australian humour is the driest in the world. It's drier than an AA clinic. We have a communal case of chronic septicaemia. Williamson's work reflects this caustic, comedic edge of ours with passion and panache. 'Poetic justice' is the only real justice in the world—and I say that married to a lawyer! We writers can always impale people on the ends of our pens. In *Soulmates* Williamson has shish-kebabed a whole host of Conan the Grammarians on behalf of all authors who've been dismissed for not plucking our highbrows. Thank you DW.

London
May 2003

P.S. Why is there no other word for thesaurus? And anyway, I thought they were extinct?

Soulmates was first produced by Sydney Theatre Company, at the Drama Theatre, Sydney Opera House, on 13 April 2002 with the following cast:

HEATHER	Jacki Weaver
DANNY	William Zappa
KATIE	Amanda Muggleton
GORDON	Barry Quin
FIONA	Deborah Kennedy
GREG	Jonathan Biggins
MAX	Sean Taylor

Director, Gale Edwards
Set Designer, Brian Thomson
Lighting Designer, John Rayment
Sound Design, Paul Charlier
Assistant Director, Annabel Scholes

CHARACTERS

HEATHER
DANNY
KATIE
GORDON
FIONA
GREG
MAX

The extract from Don De Lillo's *Underworld* on page 105 is reprinted with the kind permission of Macmillan, London, UK.

ACT ONE

SCENE ONE

Heather's house. Parkville. Melbourne. 2001.

DANNY, 45, walks in to find his wife HEATHER, 40, curled up on the divan reading a book. DANNY is wild and tousled, HEATHER groomed and very attractive.

DANNY: Hi. Good day?

    HEATHER *continues to read the book.*

Sorry I asked.

HEATHER: You should know by now that investment advisers do not *have* 'good' days. If you've made your client a packet the phone never rings, but if the market dips and shaves a half of one percent off the net worth of someone who's already on the way to their first billion…

    She shakes her head in disgust.

DANNY: Sorry I asked.

HEATHER: A client screamed at me today. 'My *last* financial adviser made my money grow, not shrink.' After fifteen minutes I finally lost it.

DANNY: You gave it to him?

HEATHER: Her. Widow in her forties worth forty-six million dollars. Never done anything more intellectually challenging in her life than book a facial.

DANNY: What did you say?

HEATHER: I told her that if I was psychic, like her last adviser obviously was, I'd have rung Osama bin Laden and made it very clear to him how much distress the September Eleven market dip was going to cause her.

DANNY: Good for you.

HEATHER: No, not good for me. I lost the client and Brian hauled me into his office and was going to fire me.
DANNY: Oh shit.
HEATHER: Oh, shit indeed.
DANNY: He didn't?
HEATHER: No. I wept.
DANNY: Wept?
HEATHER: I was down to trying anything. Get fired in my game and you're unemployable. So did *you* have a lovely day?
DANNY: Not particularly.
HEATHER: What did you do? Exactly.
DANNY: Finished the new V.S. Naipaul. Terrible. He's even more viciously snobbish about the third world than ever.
HEATHER: Didn't he just win the Nobel Prize?
DANNY: Precisely. One of the main points I'm going to make in my review is just how debased the Nobel has become.
HEATHER: Shock waves will reverberate around the world.
DANNY: Okay, we all know my magazine hasn't got a huge circulation—
HEATHER: Yes we do.
DANNY: But it's hugely influential in setting the literary agenda of this nation.

    HEATHER *continues to read.*

Whether you want to listen or not, serious literature is an endangered species.
HEATHER: [*nodding and wearily repeating his oft-quoted mantra*] Being destroyed on one hand by modish postmodernism with its message that soap opera is as relevant as Dostoevsky, and on the other by the huge marketing clout of multinational publishers flooding us with airport trash.

    She goes back to her book.

DANNY: There was a time when you were proud of what I did.

    HEATHER *continues to read.* DANNY *looks at her, angry and upset that she won't respond.*

HEATHER: You know what my dream of a perfect day is? Sitting down like you do and reading one book.

DANNY: What I do is not recreation. It's work, serious work. Serious assessment.

HEATHER: All I'm able to do is snatch a few chapters before I fall asleep exhausted.

She starts to read again. He stays standing above her and cranes his neck to try and see what it is she's reading. She looks up and sees what he's trying to do. She holds the book up to him defiantly.

Katie Best's latest. Airport trash. Shoot me.

DANNY: What you read is your business.

HEATHER: No, no. You'll very shortly make it *your* business.

DANNY: Okay, I *am* curious as to why you'd waste your time with Katie Best when there are bookshelves all over the house full of writers who make words sing.

HEATHER: Sometimes I like to read a page-turner.

DANNY: What are you saying? Works of breathtaking imaginative power *don't* make you want to turn the page?

HEATHER: Danny, I work sixty hours a week and I sometimes like to come home and read a straight-forward, linear, well-plotted *story*. Something that makes you wonder what's going to happen next!

DANNY: There goes James Joyce.

HEATHER: [*suddenly irritated*] I've tried to read *Ulysses* three times, and I finally asked myself why I was wasting my life trying to decode the incoherent ramblings of a profoundly misogynist Irish drunk! And ditto for Proust! I fall asleep every time I hear the word Madeleine!

DANNY: Would you like to take out your inability to cope with complexity on anyone else?

HEATHER: Danny, go away!

DANNY: Doesn't someone have to take a stand against the middlebrow predictability of Katie Best?

HEATHER: You haven't even read her!

DANNY: I've read the reviews!

HEATHER: Reviews, unfortunately, are written by people like you.

DANNY: Let's have no standards at all. Welcome the brave new postmodern world.

HEATHER: Until you have actually *read* Katie Best I'm not going to listen to one more word of your elitist bullying.

DANNY: The word 'elitist' won't silence me.

HEATHER: Tell me one that will.

>   DANNY *stands there, hurt.*

Go away!

DANNY: I'm sorry. I'm sorry you had a bad day.

HEATHER: [*looking up at him*] I had to totally debase myself to keep a job that I hate. Have you any idea of what that does to you?

DANNY: You don't *hate* it.

HEATHER: You need to believe that, don't you?

DANNY: You like the challenge. Doing your research, picking the winners.

HEATHER: If I gave it up it would be disastrous for you, wouldn't it? You'd have to get a real job like everyone else.

DANNY: When we first met you admired everything I stood for.

HEATHER: I'd just finished an Arts Commerce degree, thinking the commerce was only an insurance. Thinking that I'd maybe have a life in the arts too. [*She starts reading her book again, then looks up.*] You know what I'd *really* like? Two years off. Just reading like you do. Maybe then I'd have the *time* to read writers who make words sing.

DANNY: Do it then.

HEATHER: How? You earn *nothing*.

DANNY: Not quite *nothing*.

HEATHER: Nowhere near enough to keep Molly at a decent school and to allow us the occasional holiday and meal out.

DANNY: We don't need to live here in the inner city. We could sell up and invest the money and—

HEATHER: And live where?

DANNY: The bush somewhere where houses are dirt cheap.

HEATHER: With no community, no friends? How do you think Molly will react to being dumped in some forlorn outpost full of desperates?

DANNY: At least she might get to know her mother a little better.

She glares at him.

I wasn't meaning it like that.

HEATHER: Oh, yes you were. How many times have you crowed to our friends that you were the 'primary care giver'? About the day when she was six and she tripped over and cut herself and she ran to you, not me. You were there every day Molly came home from school. I couldn't be. It's as simple as that!

She throws the Katie Best book angrily on the sofa and walks off to bed. DANNY *watches her go, worried. He sees the Katie Best book sitting beside him on the sofa and picks it up. He glares at it angrily and flicks open the cover and starts to read. He emits a series of disgusted snorts of derision. Then a stifled chuckle which slips out and which he's patently ashamed of. Two more disgusted snorts, then another chuckle, accompanied by a shake of the head that indicates 'cheap laugh'. He tosses the book aside, gets up, then stops, comes back and starts to read it again. Another chuckle, rather louder this time.*

SCENE TWO

Manhattan. Upper West Side. Some weeks later.

GORDON UFFLER, *early fifties, American, walks into his apartment to find his wife,* KATIE BEST, *in a black brooding rage.*

GORDON: Hey, what's this? You've been crying.

She looks up at him and he comes closer and sits by her.

Is it something I've done?

He puts his arm around her. She shows him a clipping from a newspaper.

KATIE: Read that.

GORDON: [*reading the heading on the clipping*] The Melbourne *Age*? Someone who's been living in New York for nearly ten years is crying about something in the Melbourne *Age*? Honey, that's why you came here. To get away from that sort of shit.

KATIE: I know it's stupid. Thousands of people were incinerated twenty blocks from here, and in the grand scheme of things what's a bad crit?

GORDON: A mauling in the press *here* might be cause for alarm, but—

KATIE: You can never just cast off a country. Every time I go back I know people have been reading this sort of bile.

GORDON: Who reads the arts pages of the Melbourne *Age*?

KATIE: Everyone back there. Believe me, Gordon, there's a particular venom reserved for ex-Melburnians who get away.

GORDON: Who in the hell sent it to you?

KATIE: One of my old Melbourne 'friends'. [*She imitates the friend.*] 'Katie, I was so shocked when I read this that I agonised for daaaaays about whether to send it or not…' Yeah, right, that's why the postmark was the same date as the article—

    GORDON *takes the cutting from her and reads the byline.*

GORDON: 'Danny O'Loughlin.' Who the hell has ever heard of Danny O'Loughlin?

KATIE: [*taking it back*] Listen.

GORDON: Honey, I don't want to listen.

KATIE: No, listen, please. [*She takes a deep breath and reads.*] 'In order to try and make sense of current publishing trends I read the latest novel of Katie Best, the first Australian novelist ever to win a wide readership in the U. S. of A.. I can now see why. This is soap opera on the page. *Days of Our Lives* in print. Ms Best deploys her limited vocabulary with about as much forethought as a bricklayer cementing together yet another formulaic money-making edifice in which a story as old as time repeats itself yet again. Will Miss Frustrated find Mr Sex God? I admit I emitted one quiet chuckle when Ms Best employed her minor talent for the quick quip, but that was small recompense for time that could have been spent reading writers whose characters are understated, elusive and sensitive, not huge, cartoonish and sex-obsessed. Writers whose grasp of the infinite complexity at the heart of the human soul haunts one for days, not someone who reduces the human species to a checklist of gross appetites. I hope the air-headed Ms Best enjoys her money and five seconds of fame, but I won't be visiting her work again. Life is too short, I'm afraid, to indulge in the very minor talent of Katie Best.'

GORDON *goes across to her and hugs her as the tears start flowing again. He goes to take the cutting off her to tear it up, but she won't let it go.*

[*Angrily*] I don't expect everyone to love what I do. I know my limitations, but within them I write very, very well... don't I?

GORDON: If you didn't, no one would buy your books.

KATIE: I don't mind a critic who says 'this isn't my thing, but she has skill, she has craft.'

GORDON: You have and you know it, so why worry?

KATIE: My writing is my life. It's what I do and when someone unleashes that kind of venom it totally shocks you. Your mind can't come to terms with why anyone would hate you so much.

GORDON: Don't let him do this to you, Katie. It's what he wants.

KATIE: Okay, my characters haven't all survived Belsen, or been raped in Yugoslavia, but neither have most of us.

GORDON: The phrase you should note is 'enjoys her money'. That's the source of all that spleen. He absolutely *hates* the fact you're rich.

KATIE: I'm rich because hundreds of thousands of people enjoy what I write.

GORDON: He's a poor little cretin on the other side of the world eking out a miserable few dollars writing bile. Forget him.

KATIE: [*ominously*] I won't forget him. I never forget them. Every one of their names is etched on my brain. And I've got a long memory.

GORDON *holds out his hand for the article.*

GORDON: Katie, give it to me. I'll rip it up.

KATIE: Not until I memorise every word. Especially 'air headed'.

SCENE THREE

Manhattan. Hotel room. Midtown. A week later.

GREG GROVES, *mid-forties, watches television while his wife,* FIONA MASSEY, *late-thirties, unpacks her clothes.*

GREG: Why New York? That's all I said. A month after it's experienced the wrath of Allah. Someone with a name like Nutta al Houmous is probably arriving first class on Emirates with a nuclear bomb in his hand luggage.

FIONA: The deals are amazing. A suite in the Plaza for only five hundred Australian dollars a night.

GREG: And your purse gets stolen in the lift on the way up.

FIONA: Greg. I'll turn around and go straight home if you keep being negative!

GREG: Why didn't we just go to Port Douglas?

FIONA: We'd have a really rich cultural experience there.

GREG: There wouldn't be someone out in the corridor testing for anthrax.

FIONA: The other times we've come we've never been able to get into the good shows. This time you can get tickets for everything in town at half price.

GREG: Except for *The Producers*. Even Osama can't keep the crowds away from singing Nazis.

FIONA: Everything else. We'll have a theatrical feast.

GREG: Yes, and it adds a real edge sitting there wondering how many spores you've just inhaled.

FIONA: Last time we were here all we could get into was a monologue by that lesbian ex-porn star demystifying the vagina.

GREG: [*nodding with distaste*] Right in the front row. Still it was a huge relief to find out the G spot was a myth. All those useless hours ferreting around.

FIONA: Is *that* what you were doing?

GREG: What did you think I was doing?

FIONA: I thought you must have had a bad back. Will you stop watching that!

She reaches for the remote.

GREG: Don't! Everything but the sporting channel's George Bush. [*Imitating him*] 'By heck, those bad guys, those bad guys who come from—er—wherever they come from—they're gonna pretty soon find out—er—that we—er—we don't like bad guys. By heck, they are.' Please can we go home?

FIONA: Don't be such a wimp. We're saving an absolute fortune.

GREG: I'm stacking that against a twenty percent chance of getting out alive. Why are you always trying to save money? We're actually rich. Or quite rich. Or given the exchange rate, a little rich.

FIONA: That's what you keep telling me, but when I ask you how rich you get vague.

GREG: Because you keep threatening to send our surplus wealth off to the refugees.

FIONA: We should.

GREG: We support every damn charity except the ingrown toenail foundation. We have little children all round the world drinking clean water and growing hydroponic tomatoes because of us. What is this guilt thing you've got about the fact we've finally got a few dollars?

FIONA: It's very hard for a socialist to adjust to wealth.

GREG: It took me no time at all.

FIONA: So everyone has noticed.

She is getting increasingly irritated by GREG *watching the television.*

What *is* that sport?

GREG: Irish hurling.

FIONA: Could you do something useful? Ring Katie Best.

GREG *looks at her considering, then shakes his head.*

You were her first publisher.

GREG: She's moved onto bigger and better things.

FIONA: She owes you a debt. No one else would publish her.

GREG: Why do you want to see her? You hate her work.

FIONA: I don't hate it. It just doesn't happen to be literature.

GREG: Then why do you want to visit her? Because she's famous?

FIONA: No!

GREG: Then why?

FIONA: All right. It *is* a little bit fascinating to see how the New York rich live.

GREG: The last time they came to Melbourne, it was obvious they didn't want to see us. Especially her husband. The prick.

FIONA: She owes you.

GREG: I'm part of her past.

He continues to watch the television.

FIONA: Greg, will you turn that off and ring Katie?!

GREG: I'm trying to work out the rules.

FIONA: You don't need to know the rules. A ball, the possibility of serious injury, and you'd sit there all day.

She takes the remote, switches it off and points to the phone.

Ring Katie Best!

SCENE FOUR

Katie's apartment. Upper West Side. That evening.

GORDON *is pouring himself a drink and looking irritated.*

GORDON: Couldn't you have made some excuse?

KATIE: He published me when no one else would.

GORDON: He's tiresome, truculent and insensitive.

KATIE: Australians call it honesty.

GORDON: I know you all started out as convicts, but how long do we have to wait?

KATIE: Gordon, he's not that bad.

GORDON: Most people grow out of Attention Deficit Disorder or take tablets.

KATIE: Greg will know who this Danny O'Loughlin is.

GORDON: Danny who?

KATIE: That critic who mauled me.
GORDON: You're not still obsessing about a critic ten thousand miles away. You read what they wrote about my last movie.
KATIE: You were just one of five producers. You weren't singled out.
GORDON: At least his wife is pleasant.
KATIE: His wife is an up-herself, small-town, intellectual snob.
GORDON: What is it she does again?
KATIE: Teaches Australian Literature part-time at one of the world's truly minor universities. Needless to say my work is never so much as mentioned, let alone set on syllabuses. Elizabeth Jolley and David Malouf and that's it. Yawn, yawn.

The doorbell rings.

GORDON: Could you not do the hurling yourself at old buddies bit?
KATIE: Gordon, you're so emotionally repressed you're almost British.

GORDON *looks at her and goes to the door with a distinct lack of enthusiasm. He assumes a smile of welcome a split second before he opens the door.* GREG *and* FIONA *enter.* KATIE *accelerates towards them and gives them each a huge hug.*

It's so *great* to see you again! Why didn't you let us know you were coming? You could have stayed *here*. You still can.

GORDON *looks horrified.*

I mean it. The Australian dollar is fiscal toilet paper. Stay here.
FIONA: That's really kind, Katie, but we couldn't impose on you like that. Especially not with the trauma all you New Yorkers have just been through.
KATIE: The worst trauma is that New Yorkers have 'bonded'. The great thing about this city was that everyone used to hate each other. Now they stare into each other's eyes and everyone wants to fuck a fireman. Stay.
GREG: [*urged by* FIONA] We couldn't impose.
KATIE: [*indicating* GREG] Impose? Hey, if it wasn't for you, Greg, I wouldn't be in a position to make the offer. Gordon, that'd be fine wouldn't it?
GORDON: [*forcing it out*] Of course.

KATIE: We've got oodles of room now that Chrissie's not here. Really, I insist.
GORDON: Katie, don't press them. They've probably got a great room overlooking Central Park.
FIONA: We have actually. At an extraordinarily reasonable rate.
GORDON: [*relieved*] Marvellous hotel. The best.
KATIE: The offer's genuine. Think about it.
FIONA: How is Chrissie?
KATIE: She's getting the best of care, but I feel terrible she's not here.
GORDON: We finally had to acknowledge that she wasn't going to get any better.
KATIE: I just miss her.
GORDON: You did all you could.
KATIE: Did I?
GORDON: Of course you did.
KATIE: She understood a lot more than they said she did. I just know it.
GORDON: You did everything you could.
KATIE: [*to* GREG] So how's your wonderful Beatrice?
FIONA: Brigitte?
KATIE: Brigitte. Why did I say Beatrice? God, I'm terrible.
GREG: Since we last met she's been expelled from three more schools.
FIONA: She's fine now. She's found a school she loves. A performance- and arts-oriented special State School.
GREG: They sit round smoking dope.

    GREG *laughs loudly.*

KATIE: Sounds *great*!
FIONA: Greg, don't talk rubbish. They do drama, music, art—and she's loving it.
GREG: [*to* GORDON] We saw your movie. On the plane. I know the critics hated it, but I thought it was *great*.
GORDON: The critical response was actually quite favourable.
GREG: Not in Australia, mate. They *hated* it. They *haaated* it.
KATIE: Gordon, it was a load of crap. Admit it.

ACT ONE

GORDON: It grossed a hundred and fifty million so I guess that's some consolation.

GREG: I hear Hollywood's pulling new releases that are too violent.

GORDON: Everyone's a tad churned up at the moment.

GREG: Terrible business, but the thing that amazes me since I got here is that no one is asking why those terrorists hate you so much that they're prepared to die?

GORDON: [*tersely*] Actually we've been asking ourselves that over and over.

KATIE: And worked out it's because of Britney Spears.

GORDON: It's because they're fundamentalist fanatics who hate the most successful free society on earth.

GREG: Too easy, mate. Too easy. How many millions has American foreign policy killed in the last fifty years?

GORDON: Some might think we've been defending democracy.

GREG: And some might think you've been defending the dollar.

FIONA: Greg!

GREG: Sorry mate. Just trying to bring another perspective. Your movie, I genuinely loved it. Theta what's her name? To see her nude I'd crawl naked over razor wire.

KATIE: Don't you dare put those dangly bits of yours at risk. They're almost as impressive as Gordon's.

   FIONA *looks at* GREG.

Ooops. [*To* FIONA] I assumed Greg would have told you? It was well before you two got together.

   GREG *looks at* GORDON.

Greg, don't get embarrassed. Gordon *has* worked out by now that I didn't arrive here a virgin.

   There's an embarrassed silence.

[*To* GORDON *and* FIONA] Sorry, I can't rewrite history. It did happen. [*She points to* GREG] Him and me. Groans, yelps, moans and 'Yes, yes, yesses'. The whole ludicrous thing. Visualise it then let's move forward twenty years.

She takes GREG*'s arm.*

Greg. Danny O'Loughlin. Who the hell is he?

GREG: Danny? He's an old mate.

KATIE: An old mate?

GREG: Went to uni with him. Oh, that's right, he wrote—

KATIE: Yes.

GREG: Don't worry. Danny's a bit of a sad case. He always wanted to be a writer and now the only way he can get attention is flinging mud.

FIONA: That's not very fair, Greg.

KATIE: Why not?

FIONA: Look, I read the piece too and it was very tough. But if you put your work out for public consumption, then surely you've got to expect a range of opinions.

KATIE: As vicious as that?

FIONA: Why let it worry you? A good marketing budget can outweigh a thousand negative crits. God, how many copies has your latest book sold?

From left: Amanda Muggleton as Katie, Jonathan Biggins as Greg, Deborah Kennedy as Fiona and Barry Quin as Gordon in the 2002 Sydney Theatre Company production. (Photo: Tracey Schramm)

GORDON: Half a million.

KATIE: Which isn't of itself an artistic crime. And possibly a little more than just a marketing triumph.

GREG: [*smoothing it over*] If you think a big marketing budget will sell any old junk, you'd be wrong. It's got to be quality junk. [*To* KATIE] Don't worry about Danny. Think of him as a mosquito. Irritating but squashable.

FIONA: Greg.

KATIE: What would you call him, Fiona?

FIONA: A serious critic of serious art.

KATIE: And what exactly is that? 'Serious art'?

FIONA: Katie, you write books that are clever and witty and entertaining, but surely you'd be the first to admit that they don't change people's lives.

KATIE: I get hundreds of letters from women who tell me they do.

FIONA: In what way?

KATIE: In what way. A newfound courage to stop letting males treat them like doormats with vaginas. A profound sense of relief that they're not the only ones who mess up their life on a regular basis—

FIONA: There are degrees of messing up a life. We've all had broken hearts from time to time.

KATIE: And while it's happening it can seem pretty crucial. [*To* GREG] I'm coming back home for a promotional tour of my latest in a few months. Can I meet this Danny O'Loughlin?

GREG: Sure, but why?

KATIE: I'd like to ask him just what he means by 'serious art'.

FIONA *looks dubious, but* GREG *nods*.

GREG: Sure. He's actually quite okay if you can get through all that pomposity.

KATIE: I promise to be on my best behaviour. Just don't let him know I've read what he said about me.

GREG: No problems. Give us a call when you arrive.

KATIE: Now food. The great thing about New York is that despite the devastation downtown the dollar still brings you anything you want to your door. What sort of cuisine do you like?

GREG: Middle Eastern? Just joking.

He laughs out loud. FIONA *tries to glare him into silence but he doesn't pick up on it.* GORDON *has a very tight look on his face. It's not going to be a night he'll enjoy.*

SCENE FIVE

Melbourne. Greg's house. Some months later.

DANNY *and* HEATHER *enter.* GREG *stands there smiling.*

DANNY: Good of you to have us over, mate.

GREG: It's been too long.

HEATHER: I thought maybe you've finally decided to poison him, given the reviews he gives your authors.

GREG: No, we treasure them. Readers know that if Danny hates it it's going to be a bloody good read and sales soar.

DANNY: Good to know I'm having an impact.

GREG: Drinks. What'll it be?

HEATHER: White.

DANNY: Red.

GREG: Not opening red 'til dinner.

DANNY: Beer.

GREG: Haven't got any.

DANNY: What have you got?

GREG: White.

DANNY: I guess that settles it.

GREG: I'm protecting you. The prime cause of contemporary neurosis is too much choice. [*He laughs loudly at his joke as he pours the wine.*] St Hilary Chardonnay. Two gold, three silver. And at dinner I'll let you loose on some '94 St Hugo, four gold, six silver. Fiona'll be down shortly. She's in a shitty mood.

DANNY *and* HEATHER *look at each other.*

ACT ONE

Not at you guys. Me as usual. Katie Best's coming, by the way.
HEATHER: [*excited*] Katie Best? I love her stuff.
GREG: [*bellowing up the stairs*] See, darling? Heather loves her stuff.
FIONA: [*offstage*] Sorry. Late from work. Be down soon.
DANNY: Katie Best?
GREG: She won't have read that piece you wrote. She's in New York.
DANNY: I don't care if she's read it or not. I stand by every word.
HEATHER: Danny, will you please not pick a fight tonight?
DANNY: I'm not about to be awed by the product of a publicity machine.
HEATHER: Danny.
GREG: Mate, lighten up. She's terrific. Warm, witty, sexy—

    FIONA *appears.*

FIONA: If sexy is launching yourself at total strangers, then yes she is.
GREG: Fiona's still shitty because she found out Katie and I had a bit of a thing.
FIONA: It cleared up the mystery of why he published her.
DANNY: [*to* GREG] You had a thing with her?
GREG: Just briefly.
DANNY: She looks pretty— [*raising his eyes*] —on the dust cover.
HEATHER: Pretty what?
DANNY: Lively.
GREG: She was, mate. She was.
FIONA: Is this the kind of 'sparkling intellectual debate' we hear about when you two get together?
GREG: [*thinking*] Pretty much.
HEATHER: [*to* GREG] How's Brigitte?
GREG: We got her into an arts and performance school.
DANNY: No! That's what we're trying to do with Molly. No other school'll have her.
GREG: It's great, mate. They just sit round smoking dope and hating their parents.
DANNY: Perfect.
FIONA: Greg, will you stop that nonsense about the dope?
GREG: Well, she got me some.

The doorbell sounds. GREG *goes to get it.* KATIE *enters and gives* GREG *one of her characteristic hugs.*

KATIE: Hey! Great to see you guys.

She hugs FIONA. *Then* GREG.

You're both looking so *well*!

GREG: You're looking pretty healthy to me. This is Danny O'Loughlin and his wife Heather McFarlane.

KATIE smiles at them. They smile back.

HEATHER: It's great to meet you. I'm a real fan.

KATIE: It's nice to know someone's still reading my books in my home town.

HEATHER: Everyone I know reads them.

KATIE: Are you in publishing?

GREG: Heather's a high-powered investment adviser.

KATIE: I'm going to get to know you better. My guy still counts on his fingers.

FIONA: And Danny's our most respected stroke feared literary critic and essayist.

KATIE: A literary lion? I hope I'm not about to be devoured?

GREG: The truth is nobody takes any notice of him.

KATIE: I'm safe in any case. I'm sure no self-respecting literary pundit would waste time on me.

KATIE smiles at DANNY.

HEATHER: I think this latest is your best.

KATIE: That's so sweet of you.

GREG: So do I.

FIONA: I've been so rushed since we got back I still haven't quite got to it.

KATIE: You don't have to. I wouldn't read my books if I wasn't me.

HEATHER: Don't be so modest. It's perceptive, it's witty and it's beautifully constructed.

KATIE: I just recycle Emily Bronte with a new version Heathcliff each time. In literary circles I'd be seen as just an... air-head, wouldn't I Danny?

DANNY: I'd never use a world like that, but occasionally I do have to draw the line between entertainment and serious art.

KATIE: Of course. And if you ever feel the need to crucify me don't feel the least bit worried. What you do is *far* more important than my chick lit.

HEATHER: Katie, don't keep putting yourself down.

KATIE: Heather, you're a sweetie. You really are. My books sell. I live a good life. I'm really grateful. I am what I am. The fact that I'm looked down on by the literary establishment doesn't worry me one jot! Let's get off this topic.

GREG: If you'd all like to sit down, I've whipped up something I've never tried before.

KATIE: You cook now, Greg? Brilliant. Since when?

FIONA: Since he realised that doing what I normally do would get him ten times more attention.

GREG: Snide, dear, snide. [*To* KATIE] I wanted you to feel you'd really come home to your roots so I've done a little Tony Bilson thing, Yabbies with a truffled coulis.

They start to move offstage. GREG *shepherds them, rounding up* KATIE *last.*

KATIE: I used to catch yabbies on a string with meat tied to the end.

GREG: I was out dangling my little string all this morning.

Some time later. They're moving back in the living room, drinks in hand, relaxing after the meal.

KATIE: Greg, that was just superb.

There's a general murmur of agreement.

GREG: What's three days of meticulous preparation when gasps of delight still ring in my ears.

Despite GREG's *attempts to paper them over, there are points of disagreement that have occurred over dinner that* DANNY *in particular feels need resolving. He's more than a little drunk.*

DANNY: [*to* KATIE] I hope you didn't interpret what I was saying personally.
KATIE: Saying about what?
DANNY: That I was surprised to hear that you'd been invited to read at the Sydney Writers' Festival.
KATIE: I did a little.
DANNY: It wasn't related to you, it's a general issue. To me writers' festivals are about celebrating serious writing.
KATIE: Which mine of course isn't.
DANNY: You write very well-crafted entertainment. Which I admire.
HEATHER: I think it's wonderful that Sydney Festival has broadened its appeal beyond the snobbish confines of Melbourne.
DANNY: [*angrily*] It's nothing to do with snobbery.
KATIE: Just out of interest, Danny, what exactly is 'serious' writing?
DANNY: One, it has to be beautifully written. The words have to sing. Two, it has to take us into areas of tragic and insoluble human pain. And on both counts, Katie, I'm sorry, your writing fails.
GREG: Danny, just shut up.
HEATHER: Could you spare us a lecture?
KATIE: No, I really want to hear this.
FIONA: Danny's entitled to have his say.
DANNY: Thank you, Fiona. Thank you. It's rather nice to come to a house in which my ideas are listened to.
HEATHER: The coulis was superb, Greg.
GREG: It's rather gruesome to make, I have to warn you. You have to put all the yabbie heads under a cloth and beat them to a pulp with a hammer.
DANNY: I won't be silenced.
HEATHER: Where's that hammer, Greg?
DANNY: I'm sorry, Katie—
HEATHER: Danny, no!
DANNY: [*ignoring her*] But your words do not sing. They *do not* sing.
KATIE: Whose words do sing, Danny? [*She picks up a book from several on a coffee table.*] Don De Lillo's *Underworld*. His words sing?
FIONA: They certainly do.

KATIE: [*flicking the book open*] Can I read?

HEATHER: Katie, you don't need—

KATIE: No, this is a debate I've been dying to have. [*She opens the book, looks for a passage and reads.*] 'It was one of those days of light and scale when everything you see has the full breadth of intention.' The words may sing, Danny, but what exactly do they *mean*? Have *you* ever had one of those days when you see a bird and think to yourself: 'Hey, that bird has the full breadth of intention'. Then you go home to Heather and say: 'You know, everything I saw today had the full breadth of intention. It was one of those full breadth of intention days.' Come on, it sings, but it's gibberish.

FIONA: You can't take one sentence out of context.

KATIE: You can expect it to mean something. Fiona, name one character you can remember from the book. I've read it. I can't.

FIONA: The modern novel isn't about plot and character. A book like that exposes the underbelly of a whole culture.

KATIE: [*looking at the cover*] Yes, that's what it says here.

DANNY: [*to* FIONA] De Lillo for my money *is* too tainted with the obligatory self-reflexiveness of postmodernism.

KATIE: Well, who *is* a writer you admire?

DANNY: Unreservedly? Unequivocally? Max Van Niekerk—

KATIE: Oh, my God. Max.

DANNY: You can't pick a sentence of his that doesn't make sense.

KATIE: I give up. Max, Max, Max—the great Max.

DANNY: Max's words sing and he looks at the deepest levels of human pain and despair without flinching.

KATIE: Whereas I wallow in the insubstantial problem of finding a loving mate.

DANNY: Literature can't wallow in the momentary pain of brief heartache.

KATIE: Brief heartache? You've either been extremely lucky, Danny, or never truly been in love.

DANNY: Haven't you had any *real* experiences of deep anguish in your life and if so why *won't* you write about them?

HEATHER: For God's sake, Danny, come home!

GREG: Did anyone pick the marinade I used for the strawberries?

KATIE: Yes, I've had experiences of real anguish in my life. Like the time I got pregnant at seventeen and the bastard disappeared and I had to raise the money and find the abortionist myself. Like the time I fell hopelessly in love at twenty-three, twenty-six, twenty-eight and thirty-one, and was lied to, cheated on, humiliated and dumped by every one of them and got totally suicidal every time. It took me until thirty-three to work out that it wasn't a crime to fall in love with someone who wasn't narcissistic or psychopathic. Yes I've had anguish. Plenty of it.

DANNY: You were telling us earlier how terrible you feel about having to institutionalise your retarded daughter and the pain it's been causing you ever since. That moved me. Really moved me. Why don't you make us feel *that* kind of pain?

HEATHER: Danny!

GREG: The killer ingredient was pepper.

KATIE: Sorry, Greg. I'll have to go.

DANNY: [*to* KATIE] Sorry. I got carried away. Sorry.

He gets up and half stumbles towards KATIE *to put his arms around her, but* KATIE *shakes him off. Then faces him.*

KATIE: The reason I write what I write is that I want my readers to cope better than I did. I want them to be tougher, wittier and stronger than I ever was. And shoot me, but I actually want them to laugh. And I actually want them to like me. And I want to sell books. And I want to earn money. But the one thing I don't ever, ever want to do is put my readers through what I went through with my daughter.

She glares at him. He stumbles back.

And if that means I never get invited to your precious writers' festival then I'm glad. You go and wallow in your pain, Danny. It suits you.

She picks up her coat and before GREG *can get to her she lets herself out of the door.*

GREG: Black pepper, brown sugar and a dash of balsamic vinegar. Hands up anyone who really picked it.

No one moves.

◆ ◆ ◆ ◆ ◆

SCENE SIX

Heather and Danny's place. Much later that night.

DANNY *drunkenly tries to take his shoes off, without much luck.* HEATHER *sits stony-faced.*

DANNY: What? What? What've I done now? What?
HEATHER: What? Are you kidding?
DANNY: What? Standing up for principles? That's a crime?
HEATHER: She read what you wrote in the *Age*.

   DANNY *looks at her.*

Fiona told me in the kitchen.
DANNY: So she came for a fight and she got one. And I haven't finished with her yet.
HEATHER: [*warning*] Danny. No more hatchet jobs.
DANNY: I don't do hatchet jobs. I do what critics do. I assess.
HEATHER: She writes *comedy*, for God's sake. What's the point of beating her round the head?
DANNY: Maybe because the world by and large *isn't* comic! It's difficult and lonely and terrifying. Especially when the wife you love starts behaving as if she despises you.
HEATHER: I'm getting very tired of you judging the world from Olympian heights!

   DANNY *picks up a book and thrusts it at her.*

DANNY: Max Van Niekerk. Read it. It isn't Katie Best territory, where characters agonise when the phone doesn't ring or when their favourite dessert goes off a restaurant menu. This is an extraordinary story about people who have every right to sink into despair. Yet they don't. They endure. More than endure. They laugh, they love, they grieve, they do small human kindnesses—the whole book's a poem to human resilience and courage. It's probably the greatest novel of the last ten years. Read it on the plane.
HEATHER: Okay, okay.

   DANNY *watches her as she turns away in irritation. He slumps onto a sofa.*

DANNY: I hate it when you're away at the best of times, but it's really rough for your firm make you go to New York now.
HEATHER: They're in chaos over there. They lost three staff.
DANNY: Swear to me they're not going to make you stay on?
HEATHER: One week in London, two in New York. They swore to me.
DANNY: Phone every night. I'll be really worried.
HEATHER: I will. Come to bed.

◆ ◆ ◆ ◆ ◆

SCENE SEVEN

Katie's apartment. Manhattan.

KATIE *looks up as* GORDON *enters. She's furious. And he knows it. She's holding a fax.*

KATIE: This just arrived on our fax. What is *wrong* with this man?
GORDON: Not again.
KATIE: Listen. [*Reading the fax*] 'Our no-brain harbour city to the north has a habit of assuming that it is superior in every way to Melbourne, even claiming in a recent article that its writers' festival is the premier literary event in Australia. Are they joking? A literary festival of any substance does not invite air-headed media celebrities like Katie Best, whose career has been created by clever marketing and shameless and embarrassing self-promotion. Any festival that invites Ms Best has lost the right to consider itself anything other than a debaser of the precious coin of literary worth.'

She looks at him, her eyes blazing.

GORDON: Isn't it his *wife* who's about to arrive?
KATIE: She's fine. She's a sweetie.
GORDON: Let her know what you think of her husband.
KATIE: No. I'll get him in my own time in my own way. Once I can forgive. Twice it's war.

◆ ◆ ◆ ◆ ◆

SCENE EIGHT

Katie's apartment. Manhattan. Next day.

KATIE *is with* HEATHER. *They've just returned from depositing* HEATHER*'s suitcase.*

HEATHER: I only called because I thought we might have coffee. I wasn't expecting you to ask me to stay.

KATIE: I love it when my girlfriends stay. The last thing you marry a man for is communication. Just use this place as if it's a hotel. If you've got a free night we'll all go out together. If not, fine.

HEATHER: No, no. You do the things you have to do. I don't expect to be included in your social life.

KATIE: It's so *great* to see you. Sit down.

They sit down together on the couch.

HEATHER: Katie, the reason I wanted to have coffee was to say how embarrassed I am about what Danny did.

KATIE: Heather, Danny did it, not you.

HEATHER: I told him I'd kill him if he wrote any more, but he's got this total obsession with 'serious art'.

KATIE: Judeo-Christian culture. If I enjoy it, it must be bad.

HEATHER: I finally got to read his precious Max Van Niekerk on the plane out from Australia.

KATIE: And?

HEATHER: It's wonderful, but surely there's room in the world for what he writes and what you write.

KATIE: I like to think so.

HEATHER: Have you read it?

KATIE: God, yes. Max would never speak to me again if I hadn't.

HEATHER: You *know* him?

KATIE: Max? Of *course*.

HEATHER: I thought he was South African?

KATIE: He is, but who in their right mind would want to live there? Do you want to meet him?

HEATHER: Oh, God no. I'd be totally tongue-tied.

KATIE: Don't be stupid, he'll *love* you.

HEATHER: How did you get to meet him?

KATIE: Gordon's a film producer. The more literary the writer the more passionately they dream of the film of the book. After *The English Patient*, Michael Ondatje never had to worry about money again. You'll love him. He's absolutely gorgeous.

HEATHER: He does look striking on the book covers.

KATIE: White South Africans either look like sex gods or a cloning experiment gone horribly wrong. We'll have him round. You're just his type.

HEATHER: Oh yeah, sure. A financial adviser.

KATIE: A financial adviser who looks like Meg Ryan.

HEATHER: Katie.

KATIE: Mind you, Meg Ryan look-alikes are a dime a dozen in this town, but ones that can handle his finances—wow!

◆ ◆ ◆ ◆ ◆

SCENE NINE

Katie's apartment. A few nights later.

MAX *lounges languidly on the sofa emanating a sense of casual relaxation and command. He's charismatic and handsome and in his forties.* HEATHER *sits spellbound, drinking in every word he says on a seat across from him.* KATIE *and* GORDON *are less spellbound, but then they've heard it before.* MAX *speaks in a cultivated but pronounced South African accent.*

MAX: We white South Africans carry a lot of psychological baggage. And if you're background is Afrikaner, as mine is, you're doubly cursed. Just the sound of our accent makes white liberals still shudder all over the world. But as kids we didn't know this. We had no idea we were the pariahs of the world. How could we know? Our press certainly didn't tell us, or our parents, and in our schools we were taught that we were heroes. Descendants of the valiant Voortrekkers who ventured out onto the veldt in their covered wagons to find a place in God's heart by courage, endurance and hard work. And when the Zulu came down to take our land we fought, hugely outnumbered, but because God was on our side, we won. Then the English tried to subjugate us, and put fifty thousand of our women and children in brutal concentration camps, but eventually we won again. Were we not God's chosen children? Of course we were. God had shown us. So in my heart was this deep, deep Afrikaner's pride. Then I went abroad and suddenly discovered we were the most hated people on earth. The psychic shock was... immense. The pride turned to bewilderment, then self loathing. You spend the rest of your life trying to proclaim to the world that you're not bestial and racist. But worse, worst of all, you know that deep within you is that stubborn core of Afrikaner pride that you can never get rid of. It was planted far too strongly. So you must atone, always atone, for that darkness within.

He stares into HEATHER's *eyes. She reddens.*

HEATHER: You've more than atoned. Your latest book is— every word you write is just so exactly... right. I know that's an appallingly trite thing to say but—

MAX: Heather, that's the very best thing you could *ever* say. I spend a lot of time making sure the words are just... right.

HEATHER: It's time well spent.

GORDON: The only way I can cope with this is to get drunk.

KATIE: You're well on your way to coping very well.

GORDON: I'm still two drinks behind you.

KATIE *gives him the two-fingered salute and gets up and walks to the kitchen where she starts to open another bottle of red wine.*

HEATHER: [*to* MAX] I read that you lived and worked in a township hospital for over a year.

MAX: I didn't feel I had the right to put anything on paper until I had. Mind you, that still wasn't enough time for some. I still got criticised in some quarters for 'observing my black characters from afar'.

HEATHER: That's a stupid accusation. It's patently obvious that you got right inside their skins and cared about them deeply.

Amanda Muggleton as Katie and Barry Quin as Gordon in the 2002 Sydney Theatre Company production. (Photo: Tracey Schramm)

MAX: [*to* KATIE] Please invite more of your Australian friends.

KATIE: No way. She got on the plane a total fan of mine, but by the time she got here she's a simpering acolyte of Voortrekker, Max. [*To* HEATHER] One more word of praise and you're out in the street. Hey, that's what I should do. Live in a carton for a year and write a searingly compassionate novel about the homeless. *Boxed In*. What do you think, Max?

MAX: Cardboard is your genre, Katie.

> KATIE *hits him and there's laughter, but it makes* HEATHER *a touch uneasy.*

KATIE: Let's talk about something interesting. Me or sex.

GORDON: Neither perhaps?

MAX: Sex.

KATIE: [*to* HEATHER] The word is that if you want love's fire ignited, Max has one hell of a candle. Tempted?

HEATHER: If I wasn't happily married I'd certainly be tempted.

KATIE: Married women are Max's specialty. He can return them when he's finished.

MAX: [*to* HEATHER] Don't believe any of this. I'm a hopeless romantic.

KATIE: And I'm a Carmelite nun. Now, the place we're going will be full of *very* famous people. I'll point discreetly and spell their names with my finger. If it's a good night there might even be a few who're less famous than me, in which case they'll be doing the same to us, so don't feel guilty. No one, however, will recognise Max, because he only wins literary prizes.

MAX: [*to* HEATHER] I'm afraid she's right. Do you mind going out with a nonentity?

HEATHER: Try and stop me.

KATIE: I can see where this is heading. Why don't the two of you stay here and erogenise.

MAX: I think at this stage we'd both prefer a meal.

GORDON: Yes, can we move, please? Three minutes late and they give your table away.

KATIE: That was before September Eleven. Now they wait five and some waiters smile.

HEATHER: The food must be wonderful.

KATIE: It's terrible. But it's *hugely* expensive which keeps the fame-challenged away.

GORDON: Can we go?!

KATIE: Gordon, breathe deeply, don't panic. We're on our way.

> MAX *offers his arm to* HEATHER *and they head for the door.* KATIE *turns to* GORDON, *points to* HEATHER *and* MAX *behind their backs, and gives* GORDON *a triumphant thumbs-up sign.* GORDON *looks at her askance, but* KATIE'*s not taking any notice. Things are going according to plan.*

SCENE TEN

Katie's apartment. Next evening.

HEATHER *is sitting on the sofa looking worried as* KATIE *breezes in.*

KATIE: God, I'm a media whore. My UK publicity campaign is going to plumb new depths of tackiness and I said yes to everything. You okay?

HEATHER: Max just rang and asked me to dinner.

KATIE: So what's the long face about?

HEATHER: We got on really well last night—

KATIE: You don't say. Just how far up your thigh *did* his hand get?

HEATHER: I think I'm going to sleep with him.

KATIE: Well, of *course* you're going to sleep with him. Why do you think I introduced you?

HEATHER: I've got to go home to Danny.

KATIE: Lie.

HEATHER: I'm not good at it.

KATIE: Honestly… how can I put this without being totally offensive… of all the husbands who deserve to be cheated on, your husband is near the top of the list.

HEATHER: You saw him on a very bad night.

KATIE: Heather, the man is reading a few books a week, writing a few hundred words of venom, and sending you around the world to support his posturing. Don't you honesty get resentful?

HEATHER: Yes I do.

KATIE: Why wouldn't you? It's time to have fun.

HEATHER: I'm just not good at this sort of thing.

KATIE: You get better with practice.

> HEATHER *still looks dubious.*

Heather, there are literally dozens of women out there who would gouge your eyes out if it got them a dinner with Maxy boy.

> HEATHER *still looks dubious.*

Don't try and tell me you experience erotic nirvana with Danny?

HEATHER: No, but—

KATIE: I can take one look at a couple and know instantly whether there's an undertow of carnal delight or whether it's all over, baby. Tell me the truth.

HEATHER: It's not great.

KATIE: Now tell me the real truth. It's absolutely muff-numbingly terrible, right?

HEATHER: It's as much my fault as his.

> KATIE *sighs deeply and drags* HEATHER *up off the couch to a mirror. As she does this* GORDON *comes in from the study and overhears the rest of the scene.*

KATIE: Look at yourself. If any man couldn't get himself passionate about the person in there then he doesn't deserve her. Get out and go for it. It doesn't mean a lifetime commitment. And with Max you're not likely to get one.

HEATHER: Does he have a lot of women?

KATIE: Put it this way. If you buy a book about the joys of celibacy, you won't find his name in the index.

HEATHER: So I'm just a—

KATIE: Momentary diversion? Yes, but all you need to do is turn the tables. Think of *him* as the momentary diversion. You've seen *Aida* at the Palace, *QED* at the Lincoln Center, you've done the Guggenheim and you've had Max. And of all the male diversions on offer in New York, you've gone in at just about the top. Now stop prevaricating and go shave your armpits.

>HEATHER *looks at her, still a little unsure.*

Go! Make yourself look even more drop-dead gorgeous than you are now, and come back here in the morning in a total orgasmic daze.

HEATHER: I can't. I'll have to think up some excuse.

KATIE: Heather!

HEATHER: Do you cheat on your husband?

KATIE: I don't need to. Sex with Gordon is divine, but not so divine that I won't grab Max myself if you don't get moving.

>*She watches as* HEATHER *moves off towards the bathroom.* GORDON *enters.*

GORDON: You've sent Heather off on a mission?

KATIE: She didn't need much encouraging.

GORDON: She needed a lot of encouraging. I overheard.

KATIE: She deserves it.

GORDON: She'll fall in love.

KATIE: She's realistic enough to know that Max isn't going to disrupt his life routine for an investment adviser from Melbourne.

GORDON: Realism doesn't enter into it when two people climb into bed.

KATIE: Gordon, she hasn't had a toe-curling orgasm for at least ten years, and for a woman that attractive, that's tragic.

GORDON: Max is a bastard with women.

KATIE: I've warned her.

GORDON: That won't stop her going through hell like all the rest of them.

KATIE: She needs a jolt. How could any woman with half a brain keep on living with a bottom-feeding slime like Danny O'Loughlin?

GORDON: This is why you invited her to stay. To destroy Danny O'Loughlin.

KATIE: No. She happened to be reading Max on the plane.

GORDON: Katie, I know you want to fuck this guy over really badly, but…

KATIE: He's never going to find out.

GORDON: Unless you make sure he does.

KATIE: I'm not the daughter of Satan, for God's sake. I just want the delicious and private pleasure of knowing that his wife is going right off her brain fucking his greatest literary idol. And that she's doing it in about one hour forty-eight minutes. Yoh!

GORDON: I'm going to bed.

KATIE: Go, girl, go. Yoh!

    GORDON *looks at her, shakes his head and goes.*

SCENE ELEVEN

Katie's apartment. Next morning.

KATIE *is still working on correcting her drafts, muttering away to herself in anger.* HEATHER *comes in looking radiant.* KATIE *looks up.*

KATIE: Oh Migod, look at her.

HEATHER: Is that the new book?

KATIE: [*nodding*] I was going to ask you to read the first three chapters, but in your present state you'd say the ferry timetable was a great read. It was wonderful, right? Don't tell me. I don't want to hear.

HEATHER: Unbelievable.

KATIE: I can't stand it. I'm going to have to find a lover too.

HEATHER: I just went...

KATIE: What?

    HEATHER *shakes her head. She can't say.*

You can't say 'I just went' then nothing. You went what? Totally berserk? Crawled up the walls? Clawed the flesh off his back, or all of the above?

    HEATHER *nods her head vigorously.*

I hate you. The only consolation is that you're off home today and don't have to see this all over again.

HEATHER: He's going to come and meet me.

KATIE: Where?

HEATHER: Anywhere I can plausibly conjure up a fake conference.
KATIE: Bahamas.
HEATHER: You think?
KATIE: If you're going to fake a conference, fake somewhere worth going.
HEATHER: I've got to pack.
KATIE: I'd better help you. You're in a total daze.
HEATHER: I don't think I've ever felt like this in my life.
KATIE: Oh, come on. It can't be *that* good.
HEATHER: I was starting to feel that thing they talk about was happening. If you're a woman over forty no one sees you, no one cares. You're invisible. Suddenly I feel... not only visible again, but... adored. I feel as if I'm alive again. As if I've been given a second chance.

She bursts into tears of happiness. KATIE *hugs her.*

KATIE: Sweetie, you deserve it. You really, really do.

But there's an edge of concern in KATIE*'s voice.* HEATHER *is too euphoric to pick up on it.*

END OF ACT ONE

ACT TWO

SCENE ONE

Café/bistro. Fitzroy Street. Melbourne.

FIONA *is sitting waiting for someone. She looks at her watch in irritation. The other person is obviously late.* HEATHER *hurries in and sits down.*

HEATHER: I'm so sorry. I know how busy you are.
FIONA: It's fine. I ordered a latte for you? Okay?
HEATHER: Wonderful.
FIONA: So, what's the problem you couldn't talk about on the phone?

    HEATHER *looks down, embarrassed.*

HEATHER: I've met someone.
FIONA: Oh.
HEATHER: I had to tell someone.
FIONA: Who is it?
HEATHER: A writer.
FIONA: Oh.
HEATHER: He's extraordinary.
FIONA: Extraordinary.
HEATHER: [*unable to contain it*] It's Max Van Niekerk.
FIONA: *The* Max Van Niekerk?

    HEATHER *nods excitedly.*

  Good God. Where did you meet him?
HEATHER: Katie Best introduced us in New York.
FIONA: Was it just a one off-thing or…?
HEATHER: I'm meeting him in the Bahamas in three weeks.
FIONA: What about Danny?
HEATHER: He thinks it's a conference.

FIONA: He might check.

HEATHER: I've just got to risk it. I have to see him.

FIONA: Is this really wise? I know you and Danny have had problems, but these things can get ugly.

HEATHER: [*suddenly passionate*] What kind of a life is it when you have absolutely nothing to look forward to anymore except another day at work making money for people who are filthy rich already? I can't believe that I've actually got something to look forward to again.

FIONA: If it's something you're going to do in any case, why ask my advice?

HEATHER: I feel so guilty. I just need you to say it's okay.

FIONA: Danny isn't perfect, but—

HEATHER: Can you see how this has made me feel? Can't you see the difference?

FIONA: Yes, but how long is it going to last?

HEATHER: I don't know and I don't care!

FIONA: Then why do you need my opinion?

HEATHER: You don't approve, do you?

FIONA: For all his faults, Danny's someone special.

HEATHER: I know that but, God, try living with him.

FIONA: I know he's difficult. I mean, how many times have we sat here and decided *both* our husbands are impossible? Mine for making any compromise that he has to to make a buck, yours for making no compromises whatsoever and forcing you to earn the bread.

HEATHER: And then deriding the way I do earn it.

FIONA: At least he stands for something.

HEATHER: I know, I know, but—

FIONA: Look, Max Van Niekerk is a great writer. A great, great writer, but—

HEATHER: I know all the buts. The truth is I don't feel I've got a choice. It's called being in love. You'd do the same if it happened to you.

FIONA: I don't let it happen to me. I couldn't stand all the subterfuge and guilt.

HEATHER: I've got no choice.

FIONA: Heather, I can't just give you my blessing and say: 'I'm so happy for you'. Firstly, it's going to end badly. These things always do, and I don't want to see you hurt. And secondly, if I'm really truthful with myself, I'm jealous. Acutely jealous. I'd like to have something to look forward to too.

SCENE TWO

Greg and Fiona's house. North Fitzroy. That night.

GREG *is watching television.* FIONA *sits near him, struggling with her secret.*

FIONA: Heather's having an affair, but don't you dare tell anyone.
GREG: Who with?
FIONA: Don't you dare breathe a word to Danny.
GREG: Who with?
FIONA: Someone.
GREG: Who?
FIONA: I can't say.
GREG: That's pretty rough on Danny.
FIONA: Don't breathe a word.
GREG: Why is she doing it?
FIONA: He is difficult. He's the most totally self-absorbed man I've ever met.
GREG: He's devoted to her.
FIONA: Devoted to her? He doesn't show it.
GREG: He is, believe me. He'd be destroyed if he found out.
FIONA: Well, he's not going to find out if you don't open your big mouth, is he?
GREG: What a tart.
FIONA: [*angrily*] Frankly, I can understand it.
GREG: Explain it to me.
FIONA: When you've got nothing left to look forward to in your life, then it's not much of a life.
GREG: They're booked for a two-week holiday in New Zealand, they're about to renovate the kitchen—

FIONA: Greg!

GREG: Okay, life gets mundane. For all of us. Work becomes a grind, the spark goes out of marriage. God, when all I've got to look forward to is whether I can ultimately conquer Poulet en Demi-deuil, I'm fully aware life's challenges have grown a little thin.

FIONA: Is it any wonder some of us want to do something about it?!

GREG: What are you telling me? You want to do it too?

FIONA: If Max Van Niekerk found his way into my bedroom, then you'd have to make yourself a hell lot more interesting than you are before I'd reach for the capsicum spray.

GREG: Max Van Niekerk? *The* Max Van Niekerk?

FIONA: Oh, shit. You weren't supposed to know.

GREG: How does she score Max Van Niekerk?

FIONA: She's attractive, intelligent—

GREG: She must've bloody thrown herself at him. Tart.

FIONA: There are offers you can't refuse.

GREG: He's Danny's favourite living writer. Danny would implode.

FIONA: Keep your mouth shut and he's not going to find out.

SCENE THREE

North Fitzroy hotel. Some days later.

DANNY *and* GREG *are drinking.*

GREG: So how're things?

DANNY: Not too bad. You?

GREG: Yeah, not too bad. Glad you called.

DANNY: Well, actually I have an ulterior motive. There's a young Bosnian writer living here who's just extraordinary.

GREG: Danny.

DANNY: Read the manuscript.

GREG: I'm sure it'll be very good. What's in this for you?

DANNY: It's great writing. That's what's in it for me. The stuff in the book. She and her family have lived through it.

GREG: I'm sure they have. The problem is not many readers out there will want to live through it with her.
DANNY: How would you cope if you found out that your father had died in agony pleading for someone to kill him after his ears, nose and fingers had been cut off? Or that your sister was born as the result of a brutal rape, and your mother was on the brink of insanity out of a profound sense of shame?
GREG: I'd hate to find that out. I'd also hate to have to read it.
DANNY: The kid's only nineteen. She's a fucking prodigy.
GREG: I'm sure it's a minor masterpiece—
DANNY: It's not minor. There's nothing minor about it.

> GREG *turns away.*

Greg, you're quite happy with the fact that ninety percent of your titles are gardening and cookery books?
GREG: High *quality* gardening and cookery books.
DANNY: Greg, what the fuck's happened to you?!
GREG: It's called earning a living!
DANNY: You're prostituting your talent.
GREG: Yeah, well so would you be, mate, if you didn't have a wife that was earning a fortune.
DANNY: Jesus that's low, mate.
GREG: [*angrily*] Well, fuck it, Danny. I run a commercial enterprise. You can afford to be pure because Heather earns squillions.
DANNY: That's really low. Heather, thank God, has a vision a little bit larger than yours. She's happy to be married to someone who's drawing a line in the sand. What exactly do *you* stand for, mate, except your world trips and your cellar of vintage wine?

> DANNY *holds defiant eye contact.* GREG *looks away.*

GREG: Okay, okay. I'll publish your bloody book!

> DANNY *gives him an ecstatic bear hug.*

DANNY: Mate, you won't regret it.
GREG: What's the author's name? Not that we'll ever hear it again.
DANNY: Sefica Basic.
GREG: Okay. Get Ms Basic to ring me.

DANNY *gives him another bear hug.*

DANNY: Thanks, mate. I knew you'd come good. I was at a dinner party just last week where everyone said you were a total sellout and I was the only one who reminded them of what a force for good you'd been once.

GREG: Really big of you. So... er... how's things?

DANNY *looks at him and frowns.*

DANNY: Fine.

GREG: Heather well?

DANNY: Yeah. We're having...

GREG: What?

DANNY: A bit of a dip at the moment. Fighting a lot. Getting on each other's nerves. You know.

GREG: Yeah, it happens.

DANNY: She used to sing songs to herself. That's when I knew things were okay.

GREG: No songs?

William Zappa (left) as Danny and Jonathan Biggins as Greg in the 2002 Sydney Theatre Company production. (Photo: Tracey Schramm)

DANNY: No, and it's worrying the Christ out of me. I just get this awful feeling she's just... floating away. This conference she's going to...

GREG *looks at him.*

In the Bahamas.

GREG: Yeah.

DANNY: Sounds fishy.

GREG: Heather? No earthly way.

DANNY: From her point of view, what am I? A nothing.

GREG: Hey, come on. You're holding the line against people like... me.

DANNY: That's all I've got left, isn't it? Danny, the man who holds the line and who cares? Who cares? And do *I* really care? Do you know the only thing that gives me any real pleasure these days?

GREG: What?

DANNY: Going out in the garage and working on my Austin Healy Sprite.

GREG: Still restoring that shit heap?

DANNY: Yeah, pathetic, isn't it? In my darkest moments I even think that I could happily swap places with you.

GREG: No, you and Fiona wouldn't get on.

DANNY: You know something? This is rock bottom. A few weeks back I stayed up half the night reading Katie Best's book.

GREG: You were about to crit it.

DANNY: No, I couldn't put it down. What the fuck is going on?

GREG: It's just male menopause.

DANNY: I had that years ago. [*Shaking his head*] It's all going wrong for me, mate. The postmodern brats who control academia these days ran yet another piece ridiculing me in their cruddy little journal. According to them loyalty, compassion, courage, integrity and love are just verbal fictions we've invented to trick others into behaving more decently than we do. Welcome to the age of full-blown cynicism.

GREG: Don't get too down.

DANNY: What would be the point of staying alive in a world that had no place for loyalty or love?

SCENE FOUR

Heather's house. That night.

HEATHER *is on the couch reading.* DANNY *is sitting opposite trying to pluck up the courage to broach something.*

DANNY: [*indicating her book*] Max Van Niekerk?

>*She nods.*

Great. [*He hesitates again.*] I was talking to Greg today.

>HEATHER *looks up.*

He finally said what you've been saying. I can afford to have principles because you earn the money.

>HEATHER *looks at him.*

Do you really resent it?

HEATHER: I don't want to be working as an investment adviser for the rest of my life.

DANNY: Do you want me to throw in the magazine and try and get a job?

HEATHER: [*looking at him*] Danny, I'm making you feel guilty about doing something you love doing. That's not good for you and it's not good for me.

DANNY: Heather.

HEATHER: I can't spend the rest of my life making you feel bad.

DANNY: What's going on?

HEATHER: Nothing.

DANNY: That's 'parting of the ways' type talk. This conference in the Bahamas.

HEATHER: Yes?

DANNY: It came out of nowhere. I'd never heard you mention it.

HEATHER: I did. You weren't listening.

DANNY: I would've remembered something like that.

HEATHER: You want me to show you the conference agenda?

DANNY: Something's happening between us.

HEATHER: All that's happening is that reading a book like this just makes me so sad about all the other great books I haven't read.

DANNY: I'll earn more money. I'll do more reviews, try and get a weekly literary column.
HEATHER: I don't want you to have to.
DANNY: What are you saying?
HEATHER: Danny. I don't know what I'm saying, but just don't push me. Right?

She looks at him in such as way that he realises he'd better not.

SCENE FIVE

The Bahamas. A week later.

MAX *and* HEATHER *are lying side by side on banana lounges. Both are reading.* MAX *is chuckling.*

HEATHER: What are you chuckling at?
MAX: Katie Best's latest book.
HEATHER: Is it good?
MAX: It's superficial, shallow, garrulous and gushing. Yeah, it's great.
HEATHER: That's what I really love about you, Max.
MAX: What?
HEATHER: You're tolerant. You admit you enjoy reading her.
MAX: Only to you.
HEATHER: You'd admit that you enjoyed reading her to anyone, surely?
MAX: God, no. In the game of literary musical chairs you don't say anything that isn't image enhancing.
HEATHER: You're joking. You wouldn't admit you liked it?
MAX: I'd never even admit I'd read it.
HEATHER: Max.
MAX: If the *New York Review of Books* phoned in to ask me what I'm reading right now I'd be revisiting the great masters. And the wonderful, wonderful new novels of my heavyweight literary competitors, which I course I admire immensely.
HEATHER: Would you tell the *New York Review of Books* you were here with someone like me?

MAX: No, because you've got a husband who wouldn't be amused.
HEATHER: If I didn't have a husband.
MAX: Why wouldn't I?
HEATHER: Being associated with an investment adviser wouldn't advance you in the game of literary musical chairs.
MAX: You told me you're on the verge of reinventing yourself.
HEATHER: What if that phone call came today?
MAX: I'd say I was with a fascinating woman who, in a few years time would be doing something much more interesting than scanning share markets.
HEATHER: That might be just a dream.
MAX: I'm sure it's not.
HEATHER: Do all other top writers… nurture their image?
MAX: [*nodding*] I laugh out loud when I read their interviews. So pious. So caring. So sensitive. So incredibly, incredibly politically correct.
HEATHER: They're lying?
MAX: You bet.
HEATHER: You don't lie about your own work though, surely? How hard you work to get it right.
MAX: No, none of us lie about that. When I was there living with those dying people in the township, the thing that kept going through my mind was that I *had* to get it right. Not for just for the literary fame and prizes, but to keep my faith with some incredibly brave human beings I'd come to love and admire.
HEATHER: I'm glad. That you don't lie about that.
MAX: I still ring the hospital almost daily to talk to them. I still cry openly when I hear that another one's died. No. That, you don't lie about. But when some writer says they love some other writer's work you know they're uttering the biggest lie of all, because every writer that's any good, deep down in his soul, believes they're the greatest writer that ever lived. It's the only way you can keep going, because the type of writing that gets you on the literary 'A' list is incredibly stressful, and debilitating. Every word has to be weighed against every known alternative. Everything has to be precise and beautifully placed. You get to hate your word processor so much

that sitting down in front of it almost makes you physically ill. That's why so many of us drink. Or do other things that divert.

HEATHER: Like being here with me.

MAX: You're much more than a diversion.

> HEATHER *looks away. She's not sure she is.* MAX *realises that he needs to reassure.*

Do you think I've been this honest with every woman I've been with? With *any* woman I've been with?

> HEATHER *looks at him. She hopes he hasn't.*

Truly. There's something about you that allows me to say things I've never ever admitted before. I feel like you're a...

> HEATHER *waits.*

Soulmate.

> HEATHER *suddenly and impulsively kisses him passionately.*

SCENE SIX

Katie's place. Manhattan.

HEATHER *is flustered and upset.*

KATIE: You can stay as long as you like. For heaven's sake, it's really, really great to see you.

HEATHER: I should be back home, but I can't go.

KATIE: I mean it. Stay as long as you like.

HEATHER: I've told Danny I've just stopped over in New York to talk to people in our office here. Which is more or less true.

KATIE: Then stop worrying and sit down and tell me everything.

HEATHER: I can't go home to Danny.

KATIE: Work here. I'm sure you could get a job.

HEATHER: They've actually offered me a job.

KATIE: Say yes. Frankly, Danny doesn't deserve you.

HEATHER: I can't walk out on Molly.

KATIE: Bring her with you.

HEATHER: She would probably love it.

KATIE: You'll love it too.

HEATHER: I think I would.

KATIE: Everything important artistically or intellectually either starts here or comes here.

HEATHER: I know, I know. But I don't know what to do about Danny.

KATIE: Dump the pretentious shit. Sorry, but he is.

HEATHER: He's actually very… vulnerable at the moment. But I can't just switch off the way I feel about Max. Especially now that he's…

KATIE: He's what?

HEATHER: Shown me that it's very special for him too. He said that he felt we were… soulmates.

KATIE: Right.

HEATHER: I really think he meant it.

KATIE: Right.

HEATHER: What are you saying? He didn't?

KATIE: It's the sort of thing that tends to get said when you're in the Bahamas.

HEATHER: It wasn't like that. He was honest with me in a way he said he's never been with anyone else.

KATIE: Right.

HEATHER: You're cautioning me, aren't you?

KATIE: I'm saying what you've got going with Max is totally terrific. And you deserve it.

HEATHER: But it's not going to last?

KATIE: Who knows what's going to last?

HEATHER: I know this sounds crazy, but I just know that this one is.

KATIE: Have you told Max you want to stay on here?

HEATHER: No.

KATIE: I think you should. Before you decide.

HEATHER: I'm in love.

KATIE: Well, that's *great*. That's really, really great.

◆ ◆ ◆ ◆ ◆

SCENE SEVEN

Katie's place. Later that night.

GORDON *isn't looking happy.*

GORDON: How long is she going to be staying?
KATIE: Gordon, she's lovely.
GORDON: I'm sick of sharing my house with women with problems.
KATIE: I'd like the sort of problem she's got. A twenty-four-hour serotonin high.
GORDON: She shortly will have problems. Or Max will, when he tries to explain to Anita Helborg who this new woman around town is.
KATIE: It'll be fine. Max is not about to dump the Intellectual Love Goddess of New York for a Melbourne investment adviser. Heather will be devastated and hurt and I'll do my best to comfort her, but she'll quickly realise she really loves the loathsome Danny after all, and she'll be off home in under two weeks. I promise.
GORDON: You better be right.
KATIE: It's how these things happen.

SCENE EIGHT

Fiona's place. Melbourne. Morning.

GREG *is incredulous.*

GREG: She's staying in New York? With Max Van Niekerk?
FIONA: Well, not actually staying with him yet, but she doesn't want to come home.
GREG: So where's she staying?
FIONA: With Katie. Danny thinks she's in a hotel because he only ever rings her mobile.
GREG: Heather's in cloud cuckoo land. Does she seriously think that Max Van Niekerk is going to let her move in?

FIONA: She says Max told her they're... soulmates.
GREG: Oh Migod. Even *I* tried that one in the old days.
FIONA: Maybe the Van Niekerk thing won't last, but at least she's over there.
GREG: Over where?
FIONA: New York.
GREG: New York? Who in their right mind would want to live in New York? If the Arabs don't get you, then their own loonies will.
FIONA: I'd still rather be over there than here.
GREG: What? Than Melbourne? Voted two years in a row the most liveable city in the world?
FIONA: If you're over seventy.
GREG: Fiona, Melbourne is the city that spawned the world's greatest football code.
FIONA: Don't you ever think in one of your rare contemplative moments that if you'd chosen to get out of Australia twenty years ago you mightn't be publishing cookbooks and I mightn't be teaching in a crashingly mediocre institution?
GREG: The cancer of envy has been planted in you, Fiona. Until your best friend impaled herself on a literary legend, you loved this place too.
FIONA: Tolerated. Never loved.
GREG: New York?
FIONA: Okay, it's edgy. Sometimes I love edgy.
GREG: [*angrily*] You want edgy? I know just the man. Relocated to twinless city some time back and no doubt waiting breathless for *his* Melbourne beauty. Salman Rushdie. Edgy squared.

SCENE NINE

Dean & Deluca's. Manhattan.

KATIE *and* MAX *are having coffee.*

KATIE: 'Soulmate'?
MAX: It's the sort of thing that tends to get said in the Bahamas.

KATIE: Max, she's totally besotted.
MAX: I like her a lot. I really do, but I thought she'd understand that this was a holiday thing.
KATIE: Sure. Max Van Niekerk, a few years off a Nobel Prize, Heather McFarlane from North Fitzroy, investment adviser. And as if that wasn't enough you wheel out the ultimate killer hook. 'Soulmate'.
MAX: You encouraged her to have the affair. She told me.
KATIE: All right. Neither of us is blameless. It's time for damage control.
MAX: You've got to persuade her not to stay. If Anita gets wind of this it'll be disastrous.
KATIE: It's your nightmare scenario, isn't it? Anita finds out, drops you cold, and the whole of New York sniggers because your new companion hasn't a clue about the intricacies of literary politics, and is a total embarrassment wherever you take her.
MAX: Katie, that's not it at all.
KATIE: That's exactly it.
MAX: I don't want to hurt *either* of them.
KATIE: When you forget to tell Heather about Anita before dropping 'soulmate' into her psyche, then 'hurt' is pretty much inevitable.
MAX: Don't be so fucking self-righteous. You set this up. You encouraged it.
KATIE: I thought I was steering her towards someone who knew better than to lure beyond cure.
MAX: [*with a touch of the panics*] Katie. Just help me out here. Get her to go home.

SCENE TEN

Dean & Deluca's. Some days later.

HEATHER: He'd love me to stay, but he thinks maybe he's being selfish.
KATIE: He just wants you to think it through before you break up your marriage.
HEATHER: I know in my own heart that my marriage is over, but he wants me to be sure.

KATIE: He might have a point. You can never think quite straight in the heady atmosphere of new... attachment, new city.
HEATHER: I'm quite clear in my mind but he wants me to be sure.
KATIE: I think he's right.
HEATHER: He's coming out to Australia and we'll talk about it there.
KATIE: He's going to Australia?
HEATHER: [*nodding, happily*] He's been invited to the Melbourne Writers' Festival, so it's a perfect excuse.

> KATIE *tries to conceal the fact that she's not amused.*

SCENE ELEVEN

Dean & Deluca's. Next day.

KATIE *is furious with* MAX.

KATIE: Max, you should have finished this before she got on the plane.
MAX: I couldn't do that to her. I couldn't just say 'finish'.
KATIE: All you're doing is prolonging it into overdose territory.
MAX: I'll tell her about Anita.
KATIE: After you've spent another week in bed together?
MAX: No! What do you take me for?
KATIE: A member of the male sex, whose prime characteristic is that the onset of an erection signals the end of all human decency.
MAX: She wouldn't have agreed to go back to Australia unless I made some kind of... ongoing commitment.
KATIE: Just don't fuck up this time, Max. This started as my little vendetta so I can't afford to have it go wrong.

SCENE TWELVE

Hotel. North Fitzroy. Melbourne.

DANNY *sits there smiling to himself.* GREG *looks at him.*

GREG: So what's this *amaaazing* news?

DANNY: If you're going to be like that, you can just wait.

GREG: Come on. You're dying to tell me.

DANNY: You know who I've got as the star guest at Writers' Week?

GREG: Toni Morrison?

DANNY: Bigger. Bigger.

GREG: Don De Lillo.

DANNY: Bigger.

GREG: John Updike.

DANNY: Not quite as big. Yet. Will be. Will be. My favourite writer?

GREG: Max Van Niekerk?

DANNY: Frankly, I never thought he'd reply, but he finally gets back and says it's the one place he's always wanted to see. He's heard that our landscapes have affinities with his native South Africa. News to me. I mean, we've both got earth and we've both got sky, but if that's what he thinks, then lucky us.

GREG: That's a…

DANNY: A huge coup. Huge. Sydney and Adelaide are *furious*. This *clearly* establishes Melbourne as the big one.

GREG: That's… great.

DANNY: The downside is that the committee has two new 'anti-elitist' PoMos on it and they insisted on middlebrow ballast and invited Katie Best. I screamed and threw my arms around, but I didn't put it to the vote because I sensed I was going to lose.

GREG: She's agreed?

DANNY: Could anyone keep her away? She'd open the Wagga Flower Show if anyone asked her. What I'm going to do—and I have to say this is pretty clever because it looks like I'm being tolerant—is put her on the same platform as Max and let them debate.

GREG: On?

DANNY: Art versus commerce. He'll slaughter her.

GREG: She's got a better mind than you give her credit for. You better have a good chair.

DANNY: I'll be chair.

GREG: Totally unbiased of course.

DANNY: I'll be hideously biased. And you're going to be there too.

GREG: Me?

DANNY: Asking spontaneous questions from the floor.

GREG: On what?

DANNY: The publisher's point of view, I'll write them for you.

GREG: Get stuffed.

DANNY: Come on, you'll get kudos for publishing Sefica Basic.

GREG: Ah, that reminds me. Would you write us some blurb for the cover?

DANNY: Isn't her book brilliant?

GREG: I haven't read it.

DANNY: What?

GREG: If I read the stuff I publish I'd never get anything done. You recommended her. Give us a quote for the cover.

DANNY: With pleasure.

GREG: So, how's... er... things at home?

DANNY: Feeling a bit better. I used to have to drag Heather along to Writers' Week because she said she felt out of her depth, but now she's reading every book she can lay her hands on. And since she found out I was the one who got Max Van Niekerk to come she seems to... respect me more.

GREG: Right.

DANNY: I mean, it's not exactly cuddle-bunny time again between us, but there's a thaw.

GREG: Right.

DANNY: I... let's be frank... adore that woman. And for the first time in a long while I feel she's coming back.

GREG: Right.

SCENE THIRTEEN

Fiona's place. Some days later.

GREG *is looking morose.* FIONA *is chopping onions.*

FIONA: You could do something useful. Like top and tail those beans.
GREG: When you cook I do the cleaning up.
FIONA: I cook all the time, except when there's an audience around to gasp. Will you please do the beans?
GREG: Why does anyone eat beans? After squashes, the world's most uninteresting vegetable. At least turnips have a taste. Revolting, but a taste. Beans are like eating fat grass.
FIONA: I've said that Heather can use our holiday house.
GREG: What?
FIONA: Max is coming out the week before Writers' Week begins.
GREG: So now we're aiding and abetting this liaison?
FIONA: Heather's life's her own business.
GREG: No.
FIONA: No what?
GREG: No. They can't use it.
FIONA: I've told Heather she can.
GREG: Well, she can't.
FIONA: We won't be using it.
GREG: I don't care. Danny's an old friend and I'm not being a willing accomplice to his hurt and humiliation.
FIONA: He doesn't know a thing.
GREG: No! Absolutely no!
FIONA: Why are you so touchy about it?
GREG: Why? Because he loves her. He thinks her happy mood is because they're getting closer, when the only thing getting closer is Max. How can Heather *do* this to him?
FIONA: She deserves some—
GREG: What?
FIONA: Excitement. Before it's too late! We all deserve it now and then!
GREG: What's the message I'm getting here? That those loving encounters we still have surprisingly often for people of our age, aren't really up to much?
FIONA: It's different for women. Men can jump on—
GREG: Jump on. Since when have I just 'jumped on'?
FIONA: Maybe you should occasionally.

GREG: What?

FIONA: It might make things a little more exciting for *us*!

GREG: Sorry. Max is not going anywhere *near* our place. And top and tail the bloody beans yourself.

SCENE FOURTEEN

Hayman Island. Australia. Some weeks later.

MAX *and* HEATHER *are again sitting on banana lounges.* HEATHER *is reading.* MAX *is staring straight ahead.*

MAX: I can't believe this island. Every little hillock and blade of grass has been relocated and redesigned.

She looks at him worried.

No, no. I love it. Nature with a face lift.

HEATHER: I was trying to arrange for us to use a pretty little cottage owned by a friend, but it fell through.

MAX: I love it. And I got the Writers' Week to foot the bill. I said I was mentally and physically exhausted and they think I'm at a health farm in the Blue Mountains. Orange juice and colonic irrigation.

MAX *laughs loudly.*

HEATHER: A few of my friends know. About us.

MAX: [*alarmed*] Who?

HEATHER: Just a few friends.

MAX: Not your husband, I hope. I'm on a panel with him.

HEATHER: No, certainly not. But I just thought I'd warn you that a few of my close friends you'll meet down in Melbourne will know.

MAX: Why did you tell them?

HEATHER: I had to tell someone.

MAX *looks at her.*

You told me to come home and think. And I've thought. Just about every waking moment. I want to come to New York. I want to be with you.

There's a silence. MAX *looks away.*

And Molly wants to come too.

MAX: Molly?

HEATHER: My daughter Molly.

MAX: Heather.

HEATHER: I think it would be a really, really enriching experience for her.

MAX *looks away again.*

I've realised I love literature more than anything in the world and that if I stay doing what I'm doing I'll go crazy.

MAX: What will you do? If you come?

MAX *is silent.*

HEATHER: Don't laugh, but I really want to write. Not at your sort of level of course, but I want to try. I did quite a lot when I was younger but I couldn't persevere because the job got too demanding. But more important than anything is that I want to be with you. You were right. We're soulmates.

MAX: Heather, how long have you known me? More important, how long have you spent with me? Days and nights?

HEATHER: It's not important.

MAX: Seven, eight days and nights, and it *is* important. How can you possibly know what I'm really like?

HEATHER: I've read your books.

MAX: My books are artefacts. They're things I invent.

HEATHER: [*holding up the book she's reading*] You're trying to tell me that there's nothing of you in this? [*She reads.*] 'Now as his eyes became accustomed to the dark, Jacques began to understand the relationship between those who came and those who stayed. Between the very old stringy lady from the far edges of Soweto who arrived each day with her pail of water and her bar of precious soap, who washed the wracked skeletal body of her grandson, Nkosi Ngwasi, saying you be good soon, you see, you be good soon. No one was paid. That was the point. Poor living people were caring for poor dying people. Jacques did not like to be moved. It was an impediment to the job. But in that stinking mud hut in the township, Jacques was moved most of all by Nkosi Ngwasi. Nkosi Ngwasi was twelve years old. He would become, in Jacques' opinion, the bravest man he ever met.'

She puts the book down and there are tears in her eyes.

How is he?

MAX: Heather, Nkosi is a fictional character. The narrator is a fictional character. He's a documentary film maker, not me.

HEATHER: But Nkosi is based on someone you did get close to.

MAX: Sipho Mhlongo.

MAX looks at her.

HEATHER: Is he still alive?

MAX looks at her and looks away.

MAX: I wouldn't know.

HEATHER stares at him and frowns.

HEATHER: You ring the hospital every couple of days.

MAX: Have you noticed me ringing the hospital while I've been with you?

HEATHER: You're on holiday.

MAX: [*suddenly angry*] You can't read a book and assume it tells you anything at all about who wrote it.

HEATHER: Yes, but—

MAX: You can't. You just can't. If you come to New York with your daughter, what am I supposed to become? Her surrogate father?

HEATHER: Not if you don't want to.

MAX: Heather, I've got my own life to live. Did you think of that before you started to make all these plans?

HEATHER: I'm sorry. I didn't realise my daughter was such a big issue. I love her and I just assumed you'd love her too.

MAX: Heather, you've got some fantasy in your head about me that's not real. It's not what I am. It's nothing like what I am. [*He continues to look away.*] I haven't any idea whether Sipho is alive. I haven't called the hospital for months.

HEATHER: You don't care about those people anymore?

MAX: Writers care about one thing and one thing only. Material. Sipho was material. The hospital was material. I used it with all the skill at my disposal then moved on.

HEATHER: I don't believe that. I simply don't believe it.

MAX: Well, you'd better start.

HEATHER: [*shaking her head*] You don't write just for your own glory, Max. A book like this changes thousands.

MAX: Good. But that's not why I wrote it. Katie Best recycles old tropes for momentary celebrity and cash. My end of the market jostles for enduring reputation, and that jostling is hard, tough and incredibly vicious. There's no time and no energy to be taking on troublesome step-daughters. No time to be ringing up hospitals and enquiring after the fate of people you've already used. Unless you're as ruthless as that you'll never be a writer. Don't even bother to try.

There's a silence.

You want to know what I really am. Let me tell you. When I face my adoring public I might weep a tear or two for Sipho and even mean

Jacki Weaver as Heather and Sean Taylor as Max in the 2002 Sydney Theatre Company production. (Photo: Tracey Schramm)

it, but in the depths of my heart I can't shut out the songs of the brothers of the Veldt. God's chosen people. Whose birthright is being ripped off them by a race less intelligent, less courageous, less disciplined, less determined than we are. A race so morally feckless and unable to control their impulses that they're now dying like flies of AIDS.

HEATHER: Max, you can't really *believe* that?

MAX: Of course I don't *believe* it. My reasoning mind *hates* those vile Afrikaner songs. But there's still a part of me that wants to shout them out in defiance. And the chasm between what I think and what I feel is ripping me apart.

HEATHER: That tension feeds into your art. It's shaped this book.

MAX: No, no. This book is shaped by a formula just as iron tight as Katie Best's. Make sure your central characters are afflicted with huge dollops of undeserved misfortune and every judge of every literary prize in the world will be yours. Make them feel the sympathy and concern they've forgotten how to feel in the real world, and they'll be hugely grateful you've made them feel human again. [*He gets up and walks away. Then turns back.*] You want to know the real reason I don't want you in New York?

HEATHER *nods numbly.*

Because I am totally and appallingly single-minded. Nothing matters to me except the quest for literary immortality and if you came to New York you'd soon find out that every word I'm telling you is true. And I couldn't stand that. I couldn't stand seeing it in your eyes. Heather, you are a really decent human being. You're one of those in the bush shack that came and bathed and loved and cared. I'll go on recording other people's compassion and faking a bit myself and possibly even will end up winning that Nobel Prize, but the truth is you deserve much, much better than me. Believe me, inside this shell you think you love, there is nothing but huge ambition. Nothing.

HEATHER *stares at him, shocked.*

SCENE FIFTEEN

Katie's bedroom. New York.

KATIE *is packing up to go to Melbourne.* GORDON *is standing there reading the conference agenda. He frowns.*

GORDON: You're on a panel about 'Art and Commerce'.
KATIE: Yes.
GORDON: With Max. Chaired by Danny O'Loughlin?
KATIE: Yes.
GORDON: You're being set up.
KATIE: Of course.
GORDON: Why are you flying halfway around the world to be humiliated?
KATIE: This is a fight I have to finish.
GORDON: How? By letting the world know Danny's wife is being fucked by his all-time literary idol?
KATIE: No! By putting my case as intelligently and strongly as I can.
GORDON: And if you are totally humiliated, you're trying to tell me you've got a bomb in your suitcase and you won't throw it?
KATIE: Gordon, I don't know exactly what I'll do. If that bastard pushes me too far, it's good to know the bomb is there.
GORDON: Don't do it. You'll hate yourself.
KATIE: Thanks to Danny 'I'm so brain-throbbingly brilliant' O'Loughlin, I don't feel particularly good about myself right now.

She takes the festival program back out of GORDON*'s hands and puts it in her briefcase.*

GORDON: I'm coming with you.
KATIE: Gordon, I really, really appreciate that, but this is something I have to finish myself.

SCENE SIXTEEN

Hotel. North Fitzroy. Melbourne.

GREG *is trying to calm* DANNY.

GREG: It doesn't prove anything.

DANNY: A new swimsuit I've never seen before? Briefer than I've ever seen before. And a shopping bag with Hayman Island on it?

GREG: You've probably been there years ago and forgotten.

DANNY: The furthest I've ever got into Queensland was Surfers Paradise and that was way too far. She told me she was working in Brisbane. She's having an affair. I was going to confront her but I couldn't. If it's true, I don't want to know.

GREG: Mate, even if it was true, and I'm absolutely sure it isn't, it'll just be one of those things they've got to do to…

DANNY: To what?

GREG: To feel attractive, noticed. It's a mid-forties thing.

    DANNY *looks at him.*

DANNY: She's told Fiona.

GREG: No.

DANNY: She has, hasn't she?

GREG: No!

DANNY: How long have you known this?

GREG: I don't know anything!

DANNY: You know something. Look at you. Covering your mouth with your hand, bending over double, staring at the floor. Your body language's *screaming* deceit.

GREG: I'm a publisher.

DANNY: You know something.

GREG: I overheard a phone conversation that led me to believe that maybe… but maybe not.

DANNY: You heard what?

GREG: Don't pick at it, mate. Let sleeping dogs lie.

DANNY: They're not sleeping, they're not lying, they're fucking each other. You heard what?
GREG: It was nothing, mate. Nothing. Just something like 'You go for it'. They were probably talking about something totally innocuous.
DANNY: She does want to spend twice as much as I do on redoing the kitchen.
GREG: That's it for sure. It was *exactly* that kitchen makeover sort of tone. The swimsuit means nothing. You can buy stuff from anywhere on the Web these days.
DANNY: She does shop on the Web.
GREG: She's been surfing through resorts, seen something she likes and they've sent it in their bag.
DANNY: She does shop on the Web. She loves it. [*He nods to himself in reassurance.*] This is stupid. You're right. I've probably got no cause to worry at all and yet I can't sleep, I can't eat, I'm searching through drawers for clues, I'm steaming open her mail, I'm even raiding her email page. I feel like I'm in a Katie Best novel.

SCENE SEVENTEEN

Literary forum. Melbourne. Some days later.

DANNY *introduces the panel to the audience.*

DANNY: Art versus Commerce. Can the distinction be drawn? We're very fortunate today to have two very famous and distinguished writers, Max Van Niekerk and Katie Best.

He leads a round of applause.

It's become fashionable in this postmodern era to claim that every writer, be they termed 'serious' or 'popular', is using their writing to attain money, power or fame. Personally I find this view of the world bleak and abhorrent. I think there are writers who write because they are genuinely moved and genuinely care about human misfortune and are angered by human injustice. I consider Max Van

Niekerk to be one of these writers. On the other hand there are other writers I value like Katie Best. Writers who are skillful and entertaining. Writers who have a keen and accurate eye for the foibles they see around them in their own social class or milieu. But if I'm forced to make a value judgement, I have to observe that the human problems typically tackled by Katie in her writing are not human dilemmas of the order of severity tackled by Max. And that in the hands of lesser writers than Katie, her genre can make an already self-preoccupied, affluent, middle class gaze even more deeply into their own navels than they already do. So there you are. The chair has declared his bias upfront, so it is only just that I hand the microphone to Katie to comment.

KATIE: [*taking the microphone, with bitter irony*] Well, thank you indeed, Danny. Very fair of you to swing your knockout punch before I've even entered the ring.

DANNY: I made my views known in the interests of debate.

KATIE: You don't want debate, Danny. As usual your aim is to humiliate me. Okay, a man or woman who finds out they may be about to lose someone they love isn't suffering as much as a black South African dying of AIDS in poverty. But they are suffering, Danny, wouldn't you think?

DANNY: I don't deny it, but...

He trails off, fighting to find a coherent thought.

KATIE: But what? It's not *real* pain?

DANNY: Look, I've had my fleeting moments of heartache and insecurity. We all have, but in a world full of huge injustice we must not be self-indulgent and fall apart.

KATIE: You'd never fall apart, Danny?

DANNY: Never.

KATIE: Even if you found out your wife Heather was having an affair with someone you... deeply admired?

DANNY: [*suddenly alert*] Like who?

KATIE *really wants to throw her bomb.*

KATIE: Like... your close friend, the publisher, Greg Carter.

DANNY *swings wild-eyed to* GREG *in the audience.*

DANNY: Greg? Greg?

GREG: [*from the auditorium*] Mate, we're talking hypothetically.

DANNY: I'd punch his head in.

KATIE: That sounds a little like falling apart to me.

DANNY: All right. I wouldn't be happy. I'd be angry, depressed, maybe even briefly suicidal, but can anyone here say that this means that Max's book is not superior to Katie's?

HEATHER: [*from the auditorium*] Heather McFarlane. When I read Ms Best's books, I know that she's been through everything she writes about. She's not just an observer.

MAX: Are you suggesting I have to contract AIDS before I'm authentic?

HEATHER: No, but I would like to know if you feel the pain of the people you write about? Or are they merely, like your narrator Jacques, fuel to feed the flame of your greater glory.

DANNY: I'm sorry for jumping in here, Max, but this sort of question *really* makes me angry. What Max was 'truly' feeling when he wrote

From Left: Sean Taylor as Max, William Zappa as Danny and Amanda Muggleton as Katie in the 2002 Sydney Theatre Company production. (Photo: Tracey Schramm)

the book is totally irrelevant. He's written a book which moves *us*. That's all that counts. It doesn't matter a damn what's in the author's head, if he/she can put the right words down in the right order.

GREG: [*from the auditorium*] I'd have to agree with you, Danny. Greg Carter, CEO, Carter & Field Publishing. Take Sefica Basic, the young ethnic writer I discovered—

DANNY *looks at him, outraged.* GREG *ignores the look.*

I haven't got a clue how she was feeling when she wrote it but I know that *I* felt devastated when *I* read it. And after two Premier's Literary Prizes and a shortlisting for the Booker, I know that a lot of other people felt the same.

DANNY: Exactly. Heather, what point are you trying to make?

HEATHER: Mr Van Niekerk, how much *did* you feel for those people you based your fictional characters on?

MAX: Danny's right. If I make *you* feel for the characters it doesn't matter how much *I* felt for them, but in fact I do feel strongly for the people I'm writing about, and I certainly did in this case. They literally became family for me. And I couldn't switch them off when I finished the book. They're still with me. Every one of them. [*He bows his head.*] Every one of them.

HEATHER: In fact, Mr Van Niekerk, I read an interview with you that said you still ring them every couple of days. Is that right?

MAX: They're part of my life. They always will be.

MAX *bows his head again. There's a silence.*

HEATHER: That little fellow in the book. Nkosi. He really got to me. Was he based on a real person?

MAX: Yeah. Sipho Mhlongo.

HEATHER: How is Sipho now?

MAX: Hanging in there. Weak, but his laugh is as infectious as ever.

HEATHER: [*having reached the stage*] Sipho died four months ago.

There's a stunned silence. HEATHER *walks up onto the stage.*

I rang up the hospital to check. He's dead. They also told me, Mr Van Niekerk, that you spent less than two weeks there. And you went back to a comfortable hotel every night.

DANNY: This is still all *totally* irrelevant to the quality of the book.
HEATHER: But it *is* totally relevant to the quality of Max.

MAX stares straight ahead then gets up and walks across the platform. He stops in front of HEATHER.

MAX: Congratulations. Payback for Hayman Island, and how.

The words 'Hayman Island' galvanise DANNY. *He freezes. So do* KATIE *and* HEATHER *as they look at each other.* DANNY *turns to the audience.*

DANNY: If anyone wants to stay and discuss things fine, but as far as I'm concerned this session's over.

He gets up and walks out. KATIE *and* HEATHER *look at each other again. Damage control time. They exit in the general confusion.*

SCENE EIGHTEEN

Hotel. North Fitzroy. Soon after.

DANNY *is sitting at the bar.* KATIE *enters. He turns and looks at her.*

KATIE: I introduced them in New York. Heather had taken the trouble to read his book and wanted to talk about it.
DANNY: And Hayman Island?
KATIE: As soon as he found out she was nobody of importance, didn't want to know. He'd just seen a travel piece on Hayman Island and it seemed to him to typify all that was vulgar and artificial about Australia, then he turned his back on her.
DANNY: She humiliated him publicly because he was offhand with her once. You expect me to believe that?
KATIE: You believe what you want to. You're misreading this, Danny.
DANNY: Do you really think that because Max has been humiliated this will somehow make your work any less trivial?
KATIE: What is it that makes you hate me so much, Danny? The money, the fame? The fabulous shoes?

DANNY: Yes the money, yes the fame, yes the flow of unrelenting platitudes you peddle in every press article I read.

KATIE: We all do what we can do. Max feels no pain and can fake it. I feel real pain and can't write it. Who's the better human being, for God's sake? Get a life, boyo!

DANNY: Can't you see that what happened today is no cause to break out the champagne? Every card-carrying postmodernist will come out of the woodwork and say: 'See, Max doesn't give a damn. It all *is* just a cynical game. Life, literature, the lot.'

KATIE: Well, they're more than half right.

DANNY: No they're not. It doesn't matter whether he's the most heartless human being who ever lived. What he observed and wrote gives a lie to those who say everybody else is like he is. They're not. Don't you see that? Don't you realise that that's the larger point?

KATIE: Danny, you've got a wonderful wife who stood up to a hypocrite. Nothing more. Believe it.

> KATIE *goes.* DANNY *is left alone.*

SCENE NINETEEN

Heather's house. Parkville. Later that night.

DANNY *is sitting on the bed attempting to take off his shoes.* HEATHER *looks at him.*

HEATHER: I met him for half an hour in New York

> DANNY *holds up a shopping bag with the Hayman Island insignia on it.* HEATHER *looks at the bag. She knows the game is up.*

It's over, Danny. Believe me, it's over. You saw that.

DANNY: Yeah.

HEATHER: I was stupid enough to believe he really cared.

DANNY: And if he had, you'd be gone.

HEATHER: If he had been who I thought he was. Yes.

DANNY: So you're just here by default?

HEATHER: [*suddenly angry*] Do you think you're blameless? Do you think our marriage has offered anything much to either of us for the last ten years?

DANNY: It's offered a lot to me.

HEATHER: Well, I'd never have known, would I?

DANNY: Do you think I'd be so fucking suicidal right now if I didn't give a damn?

HEATHER: Danny, you never even noticed me. Everything was about your magazine, your literary squabbles, your losses, your wins, your pronouncements, your reviews.

DANNY: Do you think you're blameless either? Totally obsessed with your work and cold as a herring in bed at night because you 'have to have your wits about you at the office tomorrow'. As if a bit of abandoned sex was going to scramble your ability to spot a Dow Jones trend line forever.

HEATHER: You'd sleep in till midday and still think you'd done a day's work!

DANNY: If you resented that so much why didn't you tell me?

HEATHER: I did.

DANNY: If you hated your job so much you should have left.

HEATHER: And we would've lived on what? What? And what would I have done? Tried to write again?

DANNY: If that was your dream, yes.

HEATHER: Don't give me that 'follow your dream' rubbish. Even though you pushed as hard as you could with your literary mates not *one* of my stories ever got published. Why? Because they were very, very ordinary.

DANNY: So were mine.

HEATHER: I fell in love with you because I thought you were a genius. And you fell in love with me because I thought you were a genius.

DANNY: And now you think I'm what? Tell me, because I don't know anymore.

HEATHER: You're a man who wants the world to be better than it is, and I still admire that.

DANNY: But?

HEATHER: You're also a man who sets his artistic standards impossibly high so he can feel superior to just about everyone. You couldn't afford to even *slightly* enjoy Katie Best because it might make you one of 'them'.
DANNY: Did you put up *any* resistance? To Van Niekerk?
HEATHER: None at all. But it's what I do, isn't it? Latch onto a genius so it'll save me having to work out what to do with my own life.
DANNY: What *are* you going to do with your own life?
HEATHER: I'm going to keep doing what I do because I know how to do it.
DANNY: Not your working life. Us. Us.
HEATHER: Do you want there to be an 'us'?
DANNY: At this moment? No. I want to shoot you and Van Niekerk, both.

    HEATHER *sighs and sits down beside him on the bed.*

HEATHER: My mother and father were together fifty-five years.
DANNY: God, don't hold *them* up as an example.
HEATHER: I asked them why they'd fallen in love. Mum said she thought Dad was brilliant, and Dad thought Mum was 'sweet'. I asked them what they thought of each other now, and Mum said she thought Dad was an idiot and Dad said Mum was a nag. First illusions are never going to last. The question is, when the reality is revealed, is there still enough left to love?
DANNY: Is there?
HEATHER: I don't know. I honestly don't know.

SCENE TWENTY

Katie's apartment. New York. Six months later.

GORDON *is reading a sheaf of notes that he's found on a table by the sofa. He's frowning.* KATIE *comes in. He looks up.*

GORDON: Katie, no.
KATIE: They're just notes, Gordon.
GORDON: All your novels start with notes.
KATIE: It's fiction.

GORDON: And you don't think Danny and Heather will recognise themselves?
KATIE: All the details are changed.
GORDON: Oh yes. Max has become a Czech. New York has become London, and you *have* changed all the names.
KATIE: It's great material, Gordon.
GORDON: No.
KATIE: I'll show it to them both before I publish. I'm not a monster.
GORDON: The minute I appear in one of your books, that's the end.
KATIE: You've been in the last three. You're just too conceited to recognise yourself.
GORDON: So how's it going to end?
KATIE: The Heather character is going to leave the Danny character and live with a musician who's twenty years younger than she is, and have companionship, fun and great sex, and the Danny character is going to edit his journal from a garret and establish an obsessive relationship with a sex worker he can only afford once a month.
GORDON: What's happening to them in real life?
KATIE: They're still together. Heather's left her firm and is working for private clients who aren't wealthy and need expert help to retire with some dignity, and Danny's still editing his journal and restoring and selling classic vintage cars and rapidly becoming rich. If I'm deciphering Heather's code he's also using Viagra frequently, all of which is sickening and shows why art should never imitate life.
GORDON: [*still reading the notes*] I still think you shouldn't use this stuff.
KATIE: We've got dogs in Australia like you. Blue heelers. Yap at your ankles and try and steer you towards the herd.
GORDON: I'd just hate to think that the woman I loved did anything that wasn't worthy of her.
KATIE: Well, she's going to. Because she's a writer, and that's what writers do.

> GORDON *retreats towards the bedroom.* KATIE *stares at the handwritten notes in her hand, then picks up a pencil and starts correcting. She continues to work and revise as the lights go down.*

THE END

www.ingramcontent.com/pod-product-compliance
Lightning Source LLC
Chambersburg PA
CBHW042130160426
43198CB00022B/2960